To

CRYSTAL ...
What Really Happened
Revised Second Edition

nice to meet you in Crystal!

By
Roger A. Neal

Best wishes
Roger A. Neal
July 14, 2006

CRYSTAL TALE BOOKS

Additional copies may
Be ordered by contacting:

CRYSTAL TALE BOOKS
59223 Park Shore Dr.
Elkhart, IN 46517
or
www.crystaltalebooks.com

Copyright ©2002 by Roger A. Neal
Revised © 2005

Library of Congress Catalog Card Number
2005903250

ISBN: 0-9768075-0-5

Printed in the United States of America

Front Cover – "The Old Mill"
Concepta N. Waters photo

Acknowledgments

This book was made possible through the cooperation, effort, and willingness of the following people: My wife, Bonnie Neal, who was my inspiration for the development of this book; Ms. Garnett Heeter of Goshen, Indiana, for editing this book; Tom Williams, Kay Williams, and Vince Matthew Savage for their research of photos in the Marble Historical Society; Ethel Rice and Wendy Highby of the Savage Library at Western State College for their assistance in obtaining records and mining data; the staff of the Elkhart Library who corresponded with the Western State College and secured microfiche containing original editions of Crystal newspapers; Ms. Pamela Dixon of the Gunnison County Clerks Office for her location of Crystal home construction dates; the staff in the Gunnison County Office of Records and Deeds in assisting me with finding original plats, deeds, mining claims, and records of Crystal property. Cheri Moyer of Gunnison, Colorado researched Ellen E. Jack's mining claims in Crystal, Colorado..

I would like to thank the past and present residents of Crystal for their contributions to its history. I am dedicating this book to my parents, Welcome Joe Neal and Esther Fogle Neal. They loved this town and wanted to preserve it for posterity. This remains the goal of the current residents of Crystal.

Roger A. Neal

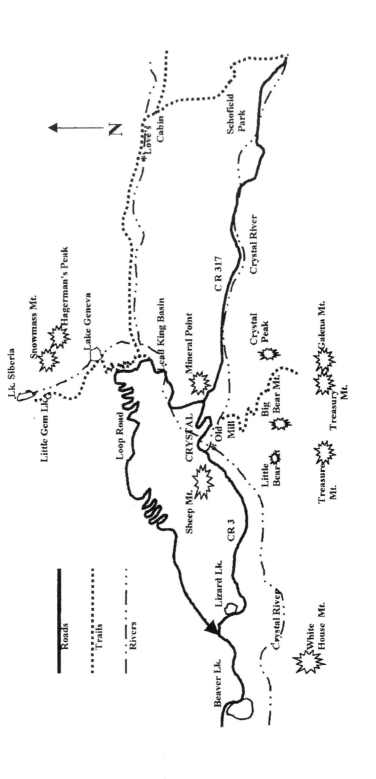

Table of Contents

PART I
THE EARLY YEARS

The Crystal Mining Camp
Begins . . .

The Ute Indians lived in the Crystal Valley until 1879. At that time they were forced from their lands by the United States Federal Government and moved to reservations in Utah. It is said that before leaving the Crystal Valley, the Ute Indians put a curse on the valley and attempted to set it on fire.

Miners then began to prospect for precious minerals, coming from Crested Butte to Gothic, Scofield, and, finally, into Crystal. Some of the miners traveled to Lead King Basin and founded the mining camp of Snow Mass.

In Crystal, tents were the first living quarters but soon gave way to log cabins or board and batten structures. Many cabins in the Scofield (today Scofield is spelled Schofield) Mining Camp were moved down to Crystal. Later, Tatum's Saw Mill was the source of building materials for Crystal.

1

Henry Kirk Saw Mill   June Kirk Blue collection

The population of Crystal has often been exaggerated. Some sources list the early years' population at about fifty. The population grew to three hundred in the summers. Many women and children wintered elsewhere. The June 24, 1881, *Gunnison News-Democrat* said there were twenty-one to twenty-two cabins in Crystal. The *Silver Lance* said that two thirds of the eligible voters did not vote in the November 1897 election. Nineteen male residents voted at that time, making the male population fifty-seven. The 1900 census lists 101 residents (includes thirty-three males over seventeen and twenty-six children). By 1910 the census listed a population of four.

Early Crystal Camp   Marble Historical Society

The prospectors usually found their ore in quartz crystallite formations. These beautiful quartz crystals provided the name for this new mining camp of Crystal. The main ores found in the Crystal Valley area included silver, lead, copper, zinc, and some gold. Due to its value, quantity, and quality, silver was the main attraction to prospectors in this valley. The Crystal River was originally called Rock Creek. However, there were many rivers in Colorado named Rock Creek so in January of 1898 the government officially sanctioned the name be changed to the Crystal River.

Following is a poem from the July 16, 1897, *Silver Lance* newspaper. This is a good description of this picturesque little mining town.

3

CRYSTAL CAMP

Crystal waters gliding onward
Toward the valleys wide and free,
Sparkling in the sunlight as they flow
Cataracts of rarest beauty.
Splashing, flashing, toward the sea,
Is the constant music that we know.
'Mid towering cliffs and grand peaks,
That caress and kiss the blue sky,
In warm reflections of beauty rare;
Where eternal snow glistening
Contrasts the verdure near by,
Is Crystal, so beautiful and fair.
                    author unknown

The town was incorporated on July 8, 1881. The town site of Crystal was plotted on about 157 acres. The town site consisted of four blocks, thirty-seven lots, three streets (Main, Center, and Sixth), and one alley. All of the lots were twenty-five by one hundred feet except two, which were thirty-five by one hundred feet. Streetlights consisted of twelve large metal encased kerosene lamps hung from poles. These lamps were lit at dusk and extinguished at 10 p.m. (since all good Crystalites were to be in bed by that time).

The four mile jack trail from Scofield to Crystal was converted into a wagon road and

4

completed in 1883. The first wagon road from Crystal to Marble was completed later.

Crystal Main Street, 1930   Robert B. Houston, Jr. collection

Some of the businesses and buildings in Crystal were the following: The two story Crystal Town Hall, blacksmith shop, schoolhouse, post office, barber shop, Colorado Trading & Development Co. (general store and rooming house), newspaper publishing and printing, town hall, Crystal River Saloon, Crystal Club Saloon, Crystal City Market, Eaton's Poultry, attorney Tom O'Bryan, Melton Jack Train, A. A. Johnson General Store, rooming house, assayer and chemist, Crystal River Stage Line, and W. A. Hogate Contractor and Builder.

Crystal Hotel, 1902   **Robert B. Houston, Jr. collection**

☞ A Full and Complete Assortment of Goods and Miners' Supplies "
Always on Hand.

HAY AND GRAIN,

Supply Store for Coal Camps and Ranch Mer.

☞ I make a Specialty of laying in Supplies
to Miners wishing to work their Prospects during
the winter.

A. A. JOHNSON,

CRYSTAL, COLO.

Branch Store at Prospect Camp.

Advertisement

A. A. JOHNSON,

DEALER IN GENERAL MERCHANDISE,

MINERS' SUPPLIES,

Powder, Caps, Fuse, Steel.

TOBACCO AND CIGARS.

Choice Groceries,

BOOTS AND SHOES,

Duck Clothing, Gloves, Socks, Underwear, Etc

Crystal River Current, Oct. 16, 1886

6

A. A. Johnson Store and Post Office   Marble Historical Society

One of the well-known and respected residents of Crystal was Mr. Albert A. Johnson. He owned and operated the general store which also housed the post office. Albert was the first postmaster in Crystal (July 28, 1882). Mr. Johnson was also the editor of the *Crystal River Current* newspaper. The first issue of the newspaper was published on October 2, 1886. Mr. Johnson was also well known for his excellent skiing ability. He often entered snow shoe (skiing) racing contests. Mail usually arrived at noon on Tuesday, Thursday and Saturday at the Crystal Post Office. Mr. A. A. Johnson and his brother Fred took turns carrying the mail from Crested Butte to Crystal over Scofield Pass. On January 1, 1890, Albert took the office of clerk for the Crystal City Council.

In 1885 J. B. Cline was appointed the first constable of Crystal.

Another notable member was Henry Maurer who worked as a blacksmith, shoeing horses and working for various mines. The blacksmith's building was on the left side of the road, about two hundred feet beyond the Old Mill as one approaches Crystal.

The Crystal River Saloon was owned and operated by Mr. A. B. Fish and William Harris. They also had mining interests together.

Ben Phillips organized the Crystal River Mining Company. Investors from the East made it possible to begin such mines as the Inez and Sheep Mountain mines. It was through the efforts of this company that the "Old Mill" was constructed in 1893.

The famous Lead King Mine was owned by George H. Tays. He was a prospector, miner, and mine owner. The *Edgerton Journal* states that in July, 1894, George carried the mail from Crystal to Gothic. George met Helen F. Phillips (Ben Phillip's sister), and they were married in 1898. Helen Tays graduated from the Denver Colorado Training School for Nurses on February 10, 1898. The people of Crystal often called upon Mrs. Tays and her nursing skills.

There were several relatives in the Williams family. Horace Williams was Ben

Phillips' brother-in-law. He and his wife came to Crystal from Caldwell, Kansas. Horace began a delivery business hauling supplies and ore. Horace also worked at various mines as a drill bit sharpener. His skill for sharpening and repairing drills was in great demand. In 1899 Horace bought the Colorado Trading and Development Company in Crystal. This general store carried staples, clothing, and all sorts of mining supplies. The general store housed the post office and in 1898 the post office began a money order business. Horace was appointed postmaster on December 3, 1900.

Ambrose Williams joined his brother, Horace, and together they ran Williams Brothers Freight. At the age of twenty-one Ambrose worked in the general store in Crystal. In 1897 Ambrose was installed as salesman-in-chief at the store. Ambrose was named the postmaster of Crystal on October 4, 1898. In the winter he would ski up and down the Crystal Valley to deliver the mail. C. Ambrose Williams' nine-foot skies are on display at the Aspen Historical Society.

Crystal Duplex (Store on left, living quarters on right)
Helen Williams on old "Duke" and
John Williams standing guard   William's family collection

The Meltons were another pioneer family in Crystal. George W. Melton wore many occupational hats. He was part owner, organizer, engineer, and superintendent of the Crystal Mountain Mining and Drainage Company. He also drove jack trains loaded with ore and supplies. Much of George's time was spent at the Crystal Mountain Mine. In 1894, George served as deputy sheriff of Crystal. George's daughter, Miss Gladys Melton, sometimes taught school in Crystal. George W. Melton's son, Charlie Melton, owned and operated jack trains to haul out ore and bring in supplies. George's daughter, Alice Melton, married Crystal resident, James Usher on

December 22, 1887. A relative, Dr. L. Melton was an investor from California. When he visited Crystal, he provided medical attention to the Crystal residents. William Melton was a miner and operated the Finley mine. William was appointed postmaster of Crystal on December 29, 1893.

George and Martha Melton   Edward Melton Fortsch collection

11

Christina Cobb operated an eating house for the miners. This eating house was located at the Crystal Mountain Mine.

James Usher was a prospector, miner, and engineer. He was elected mayor of Crystal and took office on January 1, 1890.

The Usher family with Ida Freeman   Edward Melton Fortsch collection

George C. Eaton was the editor of The Silver Lance newspaper. This newspaper took the place of The Crystal River Current on December 29, 1892. He was the treasurer of the Crystal Mountain Mining and

Drainage Company and was credited with the building of the "Old Mill." He also raised poultry to sell in Crystal. Today, a section of Crystal is named "Eaton's Addition." In November 1899 George C. Eaton was on the Republican ballot for the Gunnison County Commissioner.

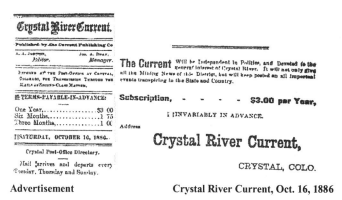

Advertisement   Crystal River Current, Oct. 16, 1886

Tom (Judge) O'Bryan was an attorney in Crystal. He did assessments, recorded patents for claims, legal work for mine disputes, and performed weddings. Mr. O'Bryan printed the Crystal newspaper when there was need for his assistance. He served as chairman of the Republican Convention in Gunnison on October 3, 1893. Tom's wife was a mail order bride from Boston. When Tom died, his wife asked Horace H. Williams to take care of the arrangements. Horace and some friends made a rough box for his coffin. Tom was then taken to the Crystal

Cemetery, where Horace said a few appropriate words and then offered a prayer. Tom and his wife provided the town with many social events. They were well respected by all the Crystal residents. Tom O'Bryan's gravestone is the only one left standing in the Crystal Cemetery (T. O'Bryan-1845-1904).

Tom O'Bryan   Edward Melton Fortsch collection

14

Tom O'Bryan Tombstone   Penny Youngman photo
Crystal Cemetery

Allen T. Hodges owned the Crystal River Stage Line. The stage line was later purchased by C. M. Hiatt and called The Crystal River Mail, Stage and Express. Mr. Hodges would substitute as a driver for the stage when called upon by C. M. Hiatt. A. T. Hodges also had a freight service for supplies. During the winter, Allen Hodges would deliver the mail by skiing up and down the treacherous canyon from Crystal to Marble and back again.

Frank W. Edgerton and his wife Rose wrote a daily journal of their experiences while living on their farm in Jerome Park and in the town of Crystal from 1886 to 1895. According to his journal, Frank was mustered into service of the Union Army in 1861. During his service in the army, he contracted measles and was hospitalized at Camp Denison, Ohio. After Frank was released from the hospital, he traveled to Jeffersonville, Indiana, and from there to Nashville, Tennessee. Frank and his command made a forced march to Pittsburgh Landing, taking part in the Battle of Shiloh and the Campaign of Corinth. During this time, Frank developed a severe case of piles (bleeding hemorrhoids), causing such extreme pain that he was unable to function. Frank was mustered out of the service at Camp Close, Ohio in 1865. He petitioned the army for a disability pension and with the aid of Tom O'Bryan, finally received his pension while living in Crystal.

In Crystal, Frank owned stock in several mines. He became an agent for the mining companies, having the power to rent, lease, or sell mining property. He also cut trees, hauled lumber, and did carpentry work for various people in Crystal. Frank spent a lot of time constructing his own cabin. His Crystal cabin is still standing today. It is known as the Sperry Cabin. The events in the *Edgerton Journal* are substantiated by the local newspapers of that time.

The Edgerton House   Edward Melton Fortsch collection

On December 2, 1891, W. P. Nelson, came to Crystal from Aspen to develop mining properties and sell stocks in them. Porter Nelson also acted as the secretary of small companies for absentee owners. Nelson owned several mining interests and purchased A. A. Johnson's General Store. Even as late as June 28, 1936, Porter Nelson continued to buy Crystal properties with the intent of developing them or selling them for a profit. Porter Nelson probably had the longest working relationship with Crystal properties, even though he was never a full-time resident. He owned property in Crystal until his death on December 24, 1946, at the age of 84.

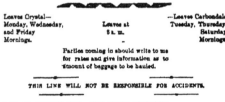

The CRYSTAL RIVER STAGE & EXPRESS LINE

Carries Passengers, Express and freight between Crystal, Carbondale and intermediate points in the valley.

| Leaves Crystal— Monday, Wednesday, and Friday Mornings. | Leaves at 8 a. m. | —Leaves Carbondale Tuesday, Thursday, Saturday Mornings. |

Parties coming in should write to me for rates and give information as to amount of baggage to be hauled.

THIS LINE WILL NOT BE RESPONSIBLE FOR ACCIDENTS.

ALLEN T. HODGES, Proprietor.

Advertisement   Silver Lance Newspaper

The Crystal Club saloon opened its doors for business on Wednesday, April 18, 1899.

Other names of prominence in Crystal were: Festus Riley, one of the stage line drivers; E. E. Fitch, the Assayer and Chemist in Crystal; W. A. Holgate, a contractor and builder in Crystal; Benjamin Totten and John Adrian operated the Crystal Barber Shop.

Social Events in Crystal. . .

The citizens of Crystal were very sociable. Socialization was especially important to the miners and their families who lived an isolated existence. The townspeople organized many clubs and activities. On June 12, 1893, Rose Edgerton wrote in her journal, *"The ladies of*

Crystal gave an ice cream, cake, and strawberry supper to benefit the Sunday School Library."

The following accounts are from The Silver Lance:

"Crystal's Christmas of 1897 will go down in the social history of the camp as the most pleasant ever observed. No shadow of want, sorrow or sickness darkened the threshold of any home or the joy of any heart. On Christmas eve the hearts of the children were made glad with many pleasing presents beautifully displayed on Charming Christmas trees, and 'children older grown' were also made glad by kindly remembrances from friends.

Christmas day was made memorable by feasts such as might have greeted Epicure at the feast of the gods on old Vesuvius.

At the plentifully laden table of Mr. And Mrs. George Melton some forty invited guests sat down to a repast replete with delicious foods, charmingly significant of the year's productions in abundance of the things, which make life worth living. Among those who were present were Mr. And Mrs. Wood, Mr. And Mrs. Edgerton, Bob and Will Brown of Marble.

At the residence of N. W. Ward, the Lead King force were guests and had a royal feast all to themselves.

Mr. And Mrs. Usher had a family dinner, at which Editor Evan Williams was their guest.

Christmas night the light fantastic was tripped until midnight—Crystalites never dance after midnight Saturday night.

Sunday Mr. And Mrs. V. A. Cobb entertained the people of the camp to the number of forty, and Mr. And Mrs. Edgerton, Evan Williams, W. G. Miller and Henry Anderson. Mrs. Cobb's elegant dinners are too well known to require any description, and indeed it would be quite impossible to do either of our Christmas feasts justice."

A NEW-YEAR'S REUNION

"The New-Year's dinner given by Mr. And Mrs. George Melton was a complete success in every respect. Most of the boys of Crystal and vicinity being present, also Mr. And Mrs. Hodges of the Penny Hot Springs, and Mr. And Mrs. Johnson, and Mrs. Livingston and daughter, Belle, of Prospect, Mr. And Mrs. Robinson of Beaver Lake, and Supt. J. W. Phillips and wife.

All partook heartily of the fat Kansas corn-fed turkey, three being devoured. Dinner was served at 4 p.m. It took William Wood some time to make George Melton understand that he came down to eat turkey and he didn't want to wait all day to be waited on. He finally was attended to by George's liberal hand, and the way turkey, pie and cake disappeared was surprising to the natives. William is a large man and judging from the amount of 'grub' he is able to store away, he must

20

be hollow to his toes, and dug out awful thin. We will match him against any one on Crystal River eating turkey and playing the 'mother of all times' on a violin.

After dinner dancing was in order. Our friend William at the bow and J. B. Cline as door manager. Every body stamped time to the 'father and mother' of all tunes until about 2 o'clock when an oyster stew was served- George Melton acting as head waiter. J. B. Cline as first assistant and James Usher as second assistant, supernumerary flunkey and general pot wrestler. Jim was the man in the right place and if he had not of been so unfortunate as to loose the string to his pole and jumping jack he would have been a source of great amusement to the crowd. After supper all enjoyed themselves by singing and dancing until daylight when everybody went home happy and wishing New-Years would come oftener."

At Thanksgiving, families would eat together. The *Edgerton Journal* states that on November 29, 1893, *"Frank went to Spring Gulch and brought home the turkey. It's weight was 11 lb. dressed. He got a can of fresh oysters to go with the turkey. There were no cranberries."*

In December of 1898 two hundred pounds of turkey were brought to Crystal for the Christmas service.

Decoration Day and July 4 were celebrated with picnics, ballgames, shooting contests, running contests, sack races, horse races, and croquet.

Sunday was a popular day for picnics and riding parties. Popular areas for picnics were the Belle Park and the Castle Kragg Park.

Dancing was a very popular activity for the people of Crystal. Dances were held regularly in the town hall. The *Silver Lance* reported that a new two story Town Hall was dedicated on July 4, 1899. The building was twenty-five feet by forty feet. It had hardwood floors and new furnishings. In her journal dated August 10, 1893, Rose Edgerton reported that Crystal had two or three dances a week. Many of the residents would also travel to Marble to attend their dance parties.

Music was an important part of their social activities. There were the Crystal River Glee Club and the Mineral Point Orchestra. The orchestra consisted of an Apollo harp, auto harp, and violins. It was noted in The *Silver Lance* newspaper as the 'string-band championship' of the mountains. The Crystal Club Town Hall was not the Crystal Club building one now sees in Crystal. The Town Hall was built first and the Crystal Club Saloon was not completed until June 1899.

Several social activities listed in the Crystal newspapers and *Edgertons' Journal* were:

(5-3-1891) *Frank Edgerton wrote in his journal, "Went to Jim Usher & Alice Meltons [sic]wedding…Brought Alice & Jim Celluloid comb and brush."*

From the *Silver Lance:*
(8-6-1897) *"At Crystal, Colorado, Wednesday, August 4th, 1897, at nine o'clock, p. m., Mr. Victor Cobb and Christina Brockaw were united in the sacred bonds of wedlock, T. O'Bryan Esq., officiating. This was the Judge's first marriage service. Mr. Cobb works in the Inez mine. The bride, for nearly a year, landlady at the eating house."*

(9-3-1897) *"People are talking about the organization of a literary and snowshoe club for the coming winter."*

(9-3-1897) *"This evening from 7:30 to 10:00 the devotees of the game will play drive whist, at the hospitable home of Judge and Mrs. T. O'Bryan."*

(11-11-1897) *"The paper flower craze has struck the women of the camp, and every table in town is decorated with varieties of flowers that do not resemble anything nature ever produced."*

(11-11-1897) *"Have you joined the Crystal Social Club? The Crystal Social Club needs you."*

23

(11-11-1897) *"Friday evening of last week Mr. And Mrs. V. A. Cobb entertained at cards. Whist, authors, high-five, and royal-casino held the interest."*

(12-3-1897) *"The flower brigade met with Mrs. Glennis Dick Usher Wednesday and held a two day's session. The Lance is expecting to receive a desk boquet [sic] soon with the compliment of the brigade."*

(12-3-1897) *"Monday afternoon, Messrs C. Ambrose Williams and Frank I. White were the guests of Judge and Mrs. T. O'Bryan at a four o'clock luncheon. The table was tastefully spread, and the service quite informal. Mrs. O'Bryan is one of those 'down-east' cooks for which New England is famed, and the guests in her dining room may be sure of a delicious repast."*

(12-31-1897) *"George Melton fed some forty guests on Christmas Day."*

(12-31-1897) *"The boys from Mineral Point make a number of grave charges against G. H. Rummel, some of which we shall not publish. They allege that in arranging to come down to camp the other day he trimmed his whiskers, put on renovated socks and otherwise arrayed himself as a masher, bent on having a gay flirtation. His conduct after*

reaching camp fully justified the boys in their opinions, but under promise of reforms we will desist from saying more at present."

(3-18-1898) "Saturday evening, the light fantastic was tripped until a late hour, vocal solos were sung, and refreshments served to Crystalites who gathered to surprise Mrs. George Melton and wish her many happy returns of her birthday."

(3-18-1898) "We failed to mention the regular meeting of the Kosy Klub which met with Mrs. N. W. Ward Thursday of last week. The passing down the street of Charley Melton with an ice cream freezer was the signal for a band of gentlemen to incidentally drop in to inspect the needlework done. A delicious lunch was then served as a tribute to the enemy and to induce them to go home. The ice cream was pronounced par excellence and the cake, - well, every woman in Crystal is an expert when it comes to making pastry."

(5-20-1898) "Last Sunday, a Sunday school was organized by some of the citizens in the school house. Mr. Ambrose Williams was elected superintendent, and three classes were formed. Seventeen were present at the meeting."

25

(6-10-1898)"The Crystal Social Club is to be a permanent organization and will retain the town hall for use through the summer."

(8-5-1898)"Saturday evening a party was given in honor of the Missouri young ladies who are guests of Mesdames O'Bryan and Usher. There was dancing at the clubroom to music of Geo. H. Rummel and Jas. Brynn until eleven o'clock."

(8-12-1898)"Saturday evening, the Crystal Club Hall was crowded with worshippers at the shrine of Terpsichore, who gathered a party complimentary to Mrs. A. T. Ferris. The dancing lasted until midnight."

(12-30-1898)"The turkey shoot passed off very nicely here last Saturday. Seven turkeys were disposed of. The winners who got one were: Al Bush, Jim Downing, Matt Downing, and Wm. Evans. Art Edgerton got three. The distance was one hundred yards and some fine marksmanship was exhibited."

(2-11-1899) "Evening snowshoe parties are the newest things in Crystal society. They are not invitation affairs, and the rules permit certain informalities, such as taking plunge baths in the snow and acrobatic turns."

(2-17-1899)"CRYSTAL SNOWBUCKER'S CLUB – The Snowbuckers Club has become a very active social organization. The officers are as follows: Norma Ward-President, Mrs. J. L. Wise-Vice President, Miss Jessie Winters-Secretary, W. B. Roddan-Official Dicker, E. E. Fitch-Superintendent Snowbucker Nursery, Jim Usher-Treasurer, W. S. Smith-Keeper of Equilibrium, A. T. Hodges-Guard of Snowbucks, T. O'Bryan-Snowshoe Statistician, U. J. Carpenter-Sliding Superintendent, Frank Dempke-Amateur's Assistant, Tom Parman-High Acrobatist, Jack Wise-Grand High Headertaker, Miss Aldean Roddan-Coasting Queen, Mrs. Usher-Mercury Messiah."

Crystal Snowshoe Club   Marble Historical Society

27

*(Canyon was spelled canon at the time of this
publication).*
*(6-2-1899)"The first party of greens gatherers of
the year came up from the canon[sic] Tuesday
with basketsful of succulent thistles."*

*(6-2-1899) "Miss Freeman treated the pupils of
the school to a picnic Decoration Day. The party,
composed of the teacher and eight pupils went
down to the Traveller's Spring, where they ate
dinner, and devoted two or three hours to
gathering bouquets and roaming through canon
scenes."*

*(6-16-1899)"W. A. Holgate announce that they
will give a dance in the new Crystal Club building,
Saturday evening June 17th, to which everybody is
invited."*

*(8-11-1899)"The Crystal checker club has been
holding regular sessions the past week or so, and
at last accounts most of the members were waiting
for their brethren to gain a reputation."*

*(8-18-1899) "WEDDING BELLS - Monday
evening, August 1, at eight o'clock at the home of
the bride's parents Mr. And Mrs. W. B. Roddan,
Rev. Read officiating, Miss Aldean P. Roddan and
Mr. Charles R. Melton were united in the sacred
bonds of Matrimony. After dinner Mr. And Mrs.
Melton were escorted to a handsome new home*

across the street, the lot deeded from Mrs. Jas. Usher, sister of the bridegroom, the building presented by his parents, Mr. And Mrs. Geo. W. Melton and the house furnishings their gift also."

(8-25-1899)"Wednesday evening at the home of Mr. and Mrs. George W. Melton a party of twenty was entertained at progressive whist…...The ladies' first prize, a handsome tidy, was won by Mrs. George C. Eaton. Mr. Lance Span received the first prize for gentlemen, a mirror. Mrs. W. B. Roddan and Mr. Frank Ira White received gentle reminders to 'ketch-up' and 'climb up' their supply of counters having run woefully short. At 11:30 light refreshments were served, after which good-nights and wishes for a repetition were said."

(8-25-1899)"Thursday evening Judge and Mrs. T. O'Bryan entertained a small number of friends to dinner, being a delightfully informal event, and pleasurable as these little affairs always are. The guests were Mr. and Mrs. Oscar Holland, of Carbondale, Mrs. R. E. Fitch, of Laramie, Wyoming, Mr. and Mrs. E. E. Fitch and Master Clyde and Mr. Frank Ira White."

Among the Mines of Crystal . . .

Silver and lead brought the miners to the Crystal valley. Some of the mines that had a great effect on the growth of Crystal were the following:

The Black Queen was patented June 29, 1898, to Crystal River Mining Company.

Lead King Mine was patented April 20, 1897, to Antoine Burnett, George H. Tays, and Winfield Smith.

The Inez was patented February 5, 1897, to Inez Gold and Silver Mining Company.

Inez Mine Stock Certificate   **Brian Levin collection**

Crystal Mountain Mine was patented to the Crystal Mountain Mining and Drainage Company.

The Daisy was patented March 3, 1897, to the Mineral Point Mining Company.

Lucky Boy was patented August 9, 1884, to the Adams Prospecting Company of Colorado.

Black Eagle was patented December 1, 1892, to Black Eagle Consolidated Mining Company.

Belle of Titusville was patented December 31, 1895, to Lute H. Pike.

The Bear Mountain Tunnel is patented, but the date is not known.

Sheep Mountain Tunnel was patented May 31, 1890, to W. E. A. Wright and Carl H. Frohn.

Sheep Mt. Tunnel Stock Certificate   Brian Levine collection

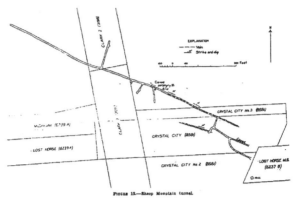

Map of Sheep Mountain Tunnel   **Geological Survey Bulletin**

In most cases, mining was made possible through investors from various parts of the country. Some of the mines were rich in ore and made money.

Crystal Mt. Mine   **Edward Melton Fortsch collection**
Steam engine house, left
Boarding house, right

Other mines were unprofitable, but the owners were hoping to strike a rich vein of ore. The following are accounts of some of the mining in the Crystal Valley as recorded in the local newspaper and the *Edgerton Journal*:

(3-26-1887) "Work upon the Belle of Titusville will in all probability be started up this spring by Mr. Copley, of Junction City, Kansas. He intends to run in the lower tunnel and push work all season, with our old friend Frances Armstrong in charge."

(4-16-1887) "A. B. Fish will shortly commence work on his Sheep Mountain property. He intends to make a trail up to the Bankers Daughter so as to make it more accessible."

(5-14-1887) "Latest quotations: Silver, $0.945 per ounce, Lead, $4.45 per hundred pounds."

(6-11-1887) "Mr. J. G. Hungerford went up to the Milwaukee, on Sheep Mountain. He expects they will do considerable work on the property this season."

(12-18-1891) Edgerton Journal…"Porter Nelson proposed the development of the Bear Mt. Tunnel, to (develop) stock of 2,000,000 shares at $1.00 per share. Nelson & Associates to Run 500,000 shares,

Edgerton, Lyons, & Molton 750,000, Treasury stock 750,000."

(7-16-1897) "Ten men are working on the Lead King doing development work, and Burnett, Smith and Tays, the owners, think the prospects excellent for striking a rich ore body."

(7-16-1897) "A small shipment of ore was taken from the Daisy, on Mineral Point last Saturday to the new smelter at Marble, by Tucker & Clark's jack train. Regular shipments from this mine commenced Tuesday."

(7-16-1897) "The repairs on the pipe line of the Belle of Titusville mine have been completed this week and the machinery will be in motion again. Two shifts of men will now be put on and as development work is being done under most favorable conditions we expect to hear of rich strikes in this property."

(7-16-1897) "Considerable work is being done on the Inez. They are running two compressed air machines, one in their upraise No. 2, extending the west drift, the other machine has just been placed near the breast of the main tunnel and will be used to prospect to the west on a very strong contact vein. The indications at this point are extremely favorable for an ore body. It is believed a small amount of work will reveal shipping ore.

Prospecting with hand steel is being done in three of four promising places in the property. This company has shipped a few cars of excellent ore during the past few weeks and the management are getting things in shape to increase the shipments."

(7-16-1897) "Some of the stockholders were visiting their properties. Among the investors were: M. V. Beiger (Mishawaka, Indiana), was visiting the Belle of Titusville."

(7-23-1897) "E. E. Kennedy (Leadville), was examining properties on Meadow Mountain; A. B. Crook, C. J. McBride, Dr. Melton, Miron Luce, and L. J. Mead (California), attended the meeting of stockholders of the Crystal Mountain Mine."

(8-6-1897) THE BELL OF TITUSVILLE STORY:

"The other day the Lance young man found his way along the miners trail up Crystal canon to the Belle of Titusville properties. We first visited the powerhouse and concentrating mill, where a water motor generates ninety horsepower, propelling the large Liner compressor. By a pipe line fifteen hundred feet long the power is communicated from the plant to the mine to propel the air drills, by means of which the great mass of stone we call Mineral Point is penetrated at the

miners pleasure, with tunnels, shafts and other passages miners call by names the tenderfoot finds a new parlance. The power plant and mill is an expansive plant of machinery, representing an investment of $30,000. The capacity of the mill is about eight tons of ore per day, and is reduced in the ratio of about four to one, varied according to the grade of the ore. To the mine is a long climb up the face of Mineral Point, following a tortuous trail that seems too steep for any other animal than man, but the sure-footed jacks travel it laden with steel and iron, powder, pipe and other mine supplies. It required nearly an hour for the writer to make the ascent from the mill, but the miners who live in the buildings near by go up in less than a half hour. The main tunnel extends into the mountain a little more than three hundred feet, following a true fissure vein, which we can see well defined by the flickering light of our candles. At the farther end of the tunnel, a room has been cut out at the side of the tunnel and here the workmen are sinking a shaft from which drifts will be run at various levels. At a depth of about twenty feet, the vein was cut and found to be increasing in width as though about to open into an ore body. When halfway in the tunnel, a strong draft of air coming from an upraise shaft, snuffed out the candles. This we were afterwards shown comes down from sixty feet above where the vein is cutout by underhand stopping along the contact for about seventy-five feet, and to a height *of about thirty feet. N. W. Ward, foreman of the mine, was very kind and explicit in explaining the theories and practice of mining. After our visit to the property, we enjoyed a pleasant hour at Mr. Ward's home and with his interesting family, partook of a splendid dinner, which Mrs. Ward prepares to perfection."*

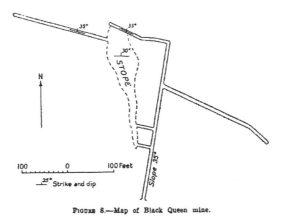

FIGURE 8.—Map of Black Queen mine.

Belle of Titusville Tunnels   Geological Survey Bulletin

(8-13-1897) THE LEAD KING STORY:

"The story of the Lead King mine covers a period of seventeen years and is another of those cases frequent in the annals of mining, where men worked almost in sight of mineral without finding it, other miners came to make other errors, and at last came the hand touched with fortunes wand or guided by knowledge gained by years of research, to wrest from nature's depository, rich stores of

mineral   In 1880, Eli Pitcher, an old prospector
located it first as the 'Ben Butler No. 1' and five
years later sold it to Al Johnson who did some
development work, but in 1894 abandoned it. The
following year, it was relocated by Andy Burnett,
W. S. Smith, and Geo. H. Tays; who christened it
'The Lead King'.   These gentlemen are all
practical miners of long experience in this district,
and the result has proved their judgment of this
splendid property correct. The mine is located at
an altitude of 10,300 feet, about one mile north of
Crystal, on Meadow Mountain. The main tunnel
is about 170 feet, cut by a shaft ninety-two feet
deep and fifty feet of upraise over the shaft to
surface, at 120 feet from the mouth of the tunnel.
Another tunnel is being driven 28 feet below the
level of the bottom of the shaft. The lower tunnel
is on the contact vein in a lime and shale contact-
one which invariably carries a strong lead of
mineral, and in this case it is a four-foot vein of
copper. The shaft in the upper tunnel is sunk on a
fissure vein which breaks up from the contact
below, and a drift being run from a fifty foot level
below the tunnel is yielding a nice lot of copper
and lead ore, taken out by underhand stoping. To
this mine the 'pay ore from grass roots' paragraph
may properly be applied, for where the lower
tunnel begins, two boulders of solid copper were
rolled out, one of which weighs a ton, and the
other a third of a ton. The first shipment of ore
from the Lead King was made about the first of

July, '96, and at present it is outputting abut five tons a day, which is being shipped as fast as it can be moved to the railroad by jack trains. A whim put in a couple of weeks ago, to hoist ore in the shaft, is the first power machinery of any description put in this property. All of the development work has been done with hand steel, and the mine has paid the cost of all development work, done by the present owners, out of its own product, and probably a little more. A short time ago, Burnett, Smith & Tays refused an offer of $75,000, spot cash for the property. It is a close company, owned exclusively by the three gentlemen, who have too good evidence of its value, to sell it for a song. The Lead King embraces three full claims, and is all patented."

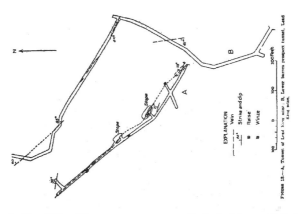

Tunnel of Lead King Mine   **Geological Survey Bulletin**

(7-30-1897) *"Yesterday afternoon the whistle at the Crystal Mountain Mine blew for the first time in twelve months. The repairs on the engine and other machinery have been completed, the power drills set up and once more the hum of activity is heard. Monday morning, six men will be put on and development work will be pushed."*

(8-20-1897) *"Tuesday the Inez closed down, pending a settlement of the financial question. The management did not feel justified in continuing operations under the present condition of the silver market. Silver is $0.51 per ounce and lead is $3.60 per hundred pounds."*

(8-27-1897) *"The Lead King is shipping a seventy-eight jack train load of ore daily, or about seven and a half tons, and breaking much more than that. One or two men will be added to the force this coming week."*

(9-10-1897) *"The Last Chance, on the east side of Crystal Mountain, is a promising mine. A one hundred and seventy-five foot tunnel penetrates this property, and an assay of ore cut into a few days ago, shows 400 ounces of silver to the ton."*

(9-10-1897) *"Last Saturday, a vein of ore eight feet wide was uncovered."*

(10-29-1897) "The Lead King tunnel is being driven rapidly. Three shifts of men are working now, and progress of several feet a day being made."

(10-29-1897) "Crystal, like many other camps in the state, is suffering because many properties in the camp are owned by persons who do not operate the mines themselves and refuse to lease to persons who would like to work such mines. Several idle properties here would be working if a lease of almost any sort could be secured."

Bear Mountain Tunnel   Geological Survey Bulletin

(11-11-1897) "The Bear Mountain Tunnel is again being worked after idled a few days and an iron formation is now being cut. The tunnel is being driven straight into the mountain, and promises to become the gateway for the mineral bodies of Bear Mountain."

(5-27-1898) "The Crystal Mountain Mine resumed work again Monday, with George Garrett in his accustomed place as machine man, and Will Brown as helper."

The Crystal Mountain Mine   Edward Melton Fortsch collection

(6-17-1898) "The men employed by the Catalpa Mining Company went out on strike last Sunday. It is alleged that the strike was the result of a cut in wages, the men having received $3.00 per day, up to the 6th of June, on which date they were reduced to $2.75 per day. It is claimed by the miners, that the mine is a wet one, and that it is customary in all Colorado camps, to pay miners of wet ground, from twenty-five to fifty cents per day, more than is paid in dry workings."

(7-15-1898) "The Laura Mine, on Meadow Mountain, was the first lode mining claim in this district for which a United States patent was issued, and lies between the Lead King and Lucky Day."

(1-6-1899) "The Crystal Mountain Mining & Drainage Company, whose big tunnel now penetrates the depths of the Crystal Mountain for some sixteen hundred feet, have reason to feel satisfied with the disclosures wrested from nature during the year just past."

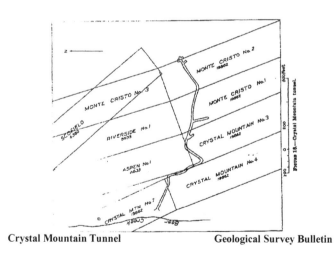

Crystal Mountain Tunnel   **Geological Survey Bulletin**

(1-27-1899) "The Denver papers were filled with errors concerning the purchase of the Lead King mine. The mine has not been sold. It was located

in 1895 and a tunnel was driven during the winter of 95-96 on a fissure vein. The smelter settlement sheets show net smelter return of about $40,000. The whole amount received from the sale of ore has been devoted to development, which consists of 750 feet of tunnels and drifts, and 175 feet of shafts and upraise in addition to surface improvements."

(10-18-1899) "This week has been one of active preparation for starting the air drills in the Bear Mountain Tunnel. The power plant has been carefully gone over, likewise the flume and pipe-line, to have everything in the best possible condition to speedily extend the big straight tunnel into the heart of Bear Mountain. Frank Dempke is to run the machine drill; Doug Kellis, Blacksmith; and George Rosetti, mucker, will constitute a part of the force."

(10-20-1899)"Three men were put on at the Burt this week and that, in connection with the new rails, ore car, and supplies hauled up, may be taken to indicate the intention of the management to push work on that property."

THE BLACK QUEEN STORY:

The Black Queen Mine was located on the south side of Sheep Mountain. The road that was used by the first prospectors to the Black

Queen is now a trail. Tons of cable, ore buckets, ore carts, timbers, machinery, all sorts of building and mining supplies, and coal were hauled by jack trains over this road. A cable was stretched from the mine, down the steep cliffs, to the Black Queen Mill, over 1,200 feet below. The mine produced about $100,000 worth of silver. From 1880 to 1892 the Black Queen was considered one of Colorado's most famous silver mines. From 1932-1934, Joe Juhan of Denver was the last recorded operator of this mine. Today the mine's entrance is covered, and the only evidence of its existence is the old brick lined boiler and the ore cart tracks protruding out of a rockslide. The following are accounts from *The Silver Lance* and *Edgerton Journal.*

(9-24-1887) "A force of six men are at work upon the Black Queen, under the management of D. D. Fowler, and a whim has been placed in position to push development work ahead as fast as possible."

In Ellen E. Jack's biography, *Fate of a Fairy,* written in 1910, she tells the story of how she became half owner of the Black Queen Mine. I was able to validate this information through First Gunnison Title and Escrow located in Gunnison, Colorado.

According to Ellen Jack (also known as Captain Jack), she leased the Black Queen to Mr. Aller. Mr. Aller had not made any

45

payments on the lease, so Captain Jack went to the Black Queen to check on her property. Upon arrival at the mine, she was surprised to see three carloads of ore, sacked and ready for shipment. Mr. Aller came out of the mining shack and told her he was surprised and hadn't expected to see her. Captain Jack responded, "By the looks of things, I don't think you did." She then informed him that the ore could not be moved until payment was made on the lease. Mr. Aller replied, "And who is going to stop me?"

Angry, Captain Jack left the Black Queen and went down the trail to the Fargo Cabin where she asked to borrow some rifles and a shot gun. The men in the cabin agreed to lend her the firearms and they helped her hide them in some brush near the Black Queen. Captain Jack and the men returned to the Fargo Cabin to spend the night. When they reached the cabin, a man from Crystal informed them about a herd of jacks and three jack punchers that would be arriving at the Black Queen the next morning.

Early the next morning, Captain Jack went to the Black Queen and waited for the jack train to arrive. Soon she could hear the ringing bells that hung around the jack's necks and the barking dogs that always traveled with them. Wearing two .44 pistols, she carried the firearms, hidden behind the brush, down to the mine and leaned them against the sacks of ore. When Mr.

Aller came to the mine, Captain Jack told him to get off her property. When Mr. Benton, the owner of the jacks, and two punchers appeared with the jack train, Captain Jack told them to turn the jacks around and get off her property.

Holding up his checkbook, Mr. Aller jumped on top of the shaft house and offered a thousand dollars to Mr. Benton if the jack punchers would take the ore. Mr. Benton blew his whistle, as a signal for his men to move the jacks forward to the mine. As the jacks started moving forward, Captain Jack shot them down. Benton started to get his gun out of his belt, but Captain Jack shot her .44. As stated in her biography, *The Fate of a Fairy,* the shot "cut off Benton's ear as clean as if by a knife." Benton threw up his hands and yelled, "I've been shot." When Captain Jack turned toward Aller, she fired another shot that hit his checkbook and took off the ends of two fingers. Benton turned the jack train around and headed for Crystal to get his wound dressed. Aller went to Gunnison where he filed charges against Captain Jack.

A trial was held in Gunnison. Mr. Aller's charges were dismissed. Mr. Benton had filed a claim for the jacks that were shot by Captain Jack, but those charges were also dismissed. Aller and Benton had to pay Captain Jack's court costs of over two hundred dollars. According to Ellen Jack, she later sold the Black Queen Mine for $25,000.

Ellen E. Jack (alias "Captain Jack")   *Fate of a Fairy*

(7-01-1889) Edgerton Journal…"Black Queen is loosening up. Mr. Johnson is in and is getting an engine up to the Queen."

(8-5-1898) "After five years of idleness, the machinery of the Crystal River Mining Company was set in motion. July 23, 1893, litigation caused the pulling of the pumps and closed down operations at the famous Black Queen Mine, known as one of the richest silver mines in Colorado. Two months ago, the last chapter of the legal controversy was ended and the company at once set preparations on foot to begin work. Ten days ago, the managers came to camp and with Resident Secretary T. O'Bryan have rushed the preliminaries to set the wheels in motion. Melton's jack train has hauled up enough coal to fuel the engine for a month. The engine has been overhauled and the fires were started yesterday and today the pumps were set in motion to un-water the mine, which will require six days steady running for the Cameron sinker and Knowles pump. Under the direction of General Manager J. P. Moore the following is the personal[sic] of the force employed: James Usher, W. F. Baringham, Bob Brown, Jim and Al Bush and two others."

(1-6-1899) "Sam Ditto, one of the young men who located the Black Queen, may be referred to as an example of Fortunes fickleness. He sold a half

interest in this property for $250. A little perseverance and stick-to-itiveness would have made him wealthy instead."

(10-20-1899) "The Black Queen is steadily taking out ore, which the jack train is packing to the Hoffman Smelter in Marble. One or two men have been added to the force and work is progressing rapidly. Coal is being packed up also, so the train is loaded both ways."

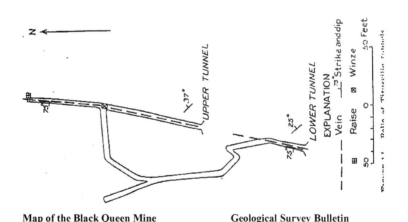

Map of the Black Queen Mine   Geological Survey Bulletin

Burros, called "jacks," hauled the ore and supplies from these mines. The jacks were tied together, forming a long line of heavily burdened animals. These lines of animals were called jack trains. Due to the poor road conditions and lack of train transportation, the jack train was the best method for delivering ore and obtaining supplies.   The following are examples of jack trains in the Crystal Valley:

(6-25-1897) "120 jacks, packed with Aspen ore, came over Maroon Pass last Tuesday. They will return loaded with a car load of sugar."

(7-16-1897) "Two heavily laden freight wagons came in from Carbondale Tuesday, one loaded with hay for the Colorado Trading and Development Company, and one bringing ore sacks to one of the mines."

(7-30-1897) "Liveryman Julian came over from Crested Butte Sunday with a four horse load of freight for the Colorado Trading Company."

(8-6-1897) "One of Clayton's jack trains brought in six tons of coal from Crested Butte Tuesday and a load of merchandise for the Trading Company yesterday."

(8-20-1897) "Jack trains from the Lead King continue with the regularity of a clock, carrying about seven tons of ore down the canon every morning."

(8-27-1897) "The Lead King is shipping a seventy-eight jack train load of ore daily, or about seven

and a half tons." * This would equate to 192 pounds of ore per burro.

(11-11-1897) "Monday Geo. Melton bought a train of sixty-four jacks from Al Annette, to haul coal and supplies to Crystal Mountain Mine."

Jack Train in Crystal   Robert B Houston, Jr. collection

(4-8-1898) "On Sunday the first jack train of the year passed through Crystal, laden with coal for the Crystal Mountain Mine. Though the train consisted of only forty animals they brought about three and a half tons of coal. The event of work being resumed, packing was of such interest that every man in Marble who could secure a horse to ride came along with the train, and we noticed Charley Melton, who owns and directs the work of the train, was ably assisted by Jim Carpenter and

Fred Rummel, both of whom seem to be developing into first-class jack punchers."

On May 27, 1898, Phil Moore and Henry Hoffman drove the first jack train of the season through Crystal on their way to the Daisy Mine.

(6-3-1898) "Yesterday afternoon, one of Charley Melton's jacks was killed by a falling tree on Lizard Lake hill, while coming toward Crystal with a load of coal."

(7-30-1898) "R. B. Wright and Jack Clayton's jack trains brought in six tons of coal from Crested Butte Tuesday and a load of merchandise for the Trading Company yesterday."

(7-14-1899) "Jacks have become very popular for riding purposes of late."

(7-28-1899) "The Eaton jack train of riding animals has been equipped with new bridles, blankets and surcingles, and look as fine as a circus outfit."

Even though the jacks were perfect for the mountain trails, heavy freight wagons were also used to bring supplies to Crystal. These supplies were for the stores, people, and mines. The wagons were usually not used to haul the ore

to the smelters because of the steep inclines and poor road conditions.

The road from Marble to Scofield was constantly in need of repair. Crystal was located right in the middle of this dangerous stretch of road. Snow slides blocked the road in the winter, floods washed out the road in the spring, mudslides blocked the road in the summer, and rockslides blocked the road continually. The people of Crystal said there were three seasons in the Elk Mountains: Winter, May and June, and the Rainy Period.

The Old Mill   **Marble Historical Society**
(Sheep Mt. Tunnel Power Plant & Dam),

The Old Mill   Marble Historical Society
(Sheep Mt. Tunnel Power Plant, left , Mill right)

History of the OLD MILL. . .

The Old Mill was constructed in 1893 and is still located at the intersection of the Crystal River and the North Fork River. The mill site on which it stands is the Lost Horse Millsite. As one views the mill, he is standing on the dump of the Sheep Mountain Tunnel Mine. Before that mine was opened, old maps show a very large pool at the base of the falls, actually the size of a small lake; but this has been filled by the tailings from the tunnel. The square superstructure in front of the building is called a vertical penstock. It contained a vertical axle, and at the bottom of this penstock was a horizontal wooden wheel. When the Old Mill was in operation, a dam was built across the river. The water was diverted down a flume through the penstock to turn the horizontal wheel. The wheel turned the vertical

55

axle and provided the power to turn the air compressor that was housed in the twenty by fifty foot building. A rusted pipe is still visible protruding from the dump through which air was piped to the Sheep Mountain Tunnel. This air powered the drills used to make holes for the placement of dynamite. The air from the compressor was also used to operate the drills in the Bear Mountain Tunnel. The building in ruin to the right of the Old Mill was the stamping mill, which had Wilfley tables for sorting ore. A bridge was constructed between the Old Mill and stamping mill so ore could be delivered, crushed, and then taken to the smelter.

The Old Mill   June Kirk Blue collection
(Sheep Mt. Tunnel Power plant,
North side view)

56

The Old Mill   **June Kirk Blue collection**
(Sheep Mt. Tunnel Power Plant)

Sheep Mt. Tunnel Power Plant, left   Robert B. Houston, Jr. collection
Mill, right

57

Accidents, Disease, and Death in Crystal's Early Days. . .

The following accounts are from the *Crystal River Current* and the *Silver Lance* newspapers:

Mine Explosion...
(1-8-1887) "J. G. Sanbourgh (an old man) was found nearly dead after setting off giant powder in his mine: J. G. Sanbough went back into the mine. While digging, he hit an unexploded cap and charge, which exploded. The old man then crawled up a ladder out of his mine and made his way back to his cabin. He thought no one would find him and had lain down to die. Fred Johnson happened by, made a fire and summoned help."

(1-22-1887) "J. G. Sanbourgh is improving nicely under the care of Mr./Mrs. Wm. Robinson."

(1-29-1887) "Three pieces of rock were taken out of J. G. Sanbourgh's cheek. One of the rocks was three inches in diameter. The old man had been complaining about pain in his cheek. The rocks could only be seen on the inside of his mouth. Eight teeth had been lost in the accident and it was thought the impact of these rocks had caused the damage. Upon removal of the rocks, a large hole was left in his cheek and something had to be held

over the hole when he ate or drank. He was able to see fine out of both eyes."

(2-19-1887) The *Crystal River Current* points out that J. G. Sanbourgh had many friends that promised to help him if asked. They had been asked to help several times, but no one offered help in any way. One of his friends promised to hold the old man's money for him, but the doctor still was not paid and his fee was now $125. Friends were asked to help take him to Crested Butte.

(2-26-1887) "J. G. Sanbourgh was carried to Scofield by four of his friends. He will be taken to Crested Butte for medical attention."

(6-18-1887) "J. G. Sanbourgh has attempted to go back to work. His left hand and thumb of his right hand were amputated. The right hand is crippled. He has partial sight in his left eye."

(6-25-1887) "J. G. Sanbourgh returned from the county hospital in Gunnison and is thankful to Dr. Grassmuck for his care. The old man intends going to work on his property, but has only partial use of his right hand and an attachment on the left arm, which he expects can be used in his work."

(7-2-1887) "J. G. Sanbourgh is running his cross-cut tunnel at the lower end of Sheep Mountain,

but finds it hard work as he has not very good use of the appliance on his left arm. J. G. Sanbourgh has brought in another partner from Gunnison to help drive his crosscut tunnel."

(12-31-1887) "Gus Bowman and Old Man Sanbourgh crossed over the range to Crested Butte for the old man to take the train to a lower level."

The Crystal River Claims Lives...
(6-4-1887) Mr. and Mrs. Andy Johnson lost their two dear children, Edna, three years old, and a seven-month-old baby while trying to cross the river in their wagon. The force of the raging river turned the wagon over, resulting in the drowning of their children. A search party was sent out and the baby was found in a pile of driftwood. They did not find the body of Edna until the water receded.

(7-30-1887) "Last Monday a search party went out to make another search for the remains of Andy Johnson's little daughter, Edna, who was drowned in the river last May. The party returned in a short time, having found her caught in a drift pile about a mile below the old ford. Her remains were brought to Prospect and buried alongside the little baby."

Mining Accident...
(6-11-1887) "Jim Usher had the misfortune to run a pick into his foot the other day which laid him up for a few days."

The Dark Angel...
(12-01-1889) The *Edgerton Journal* reported that Hortz Black died in Crystal of pneumonia.

The Edgerton Journal:
(10-29-1891) "Johnsons baby died this morning at 5 A. M. Fish and I went to the Buttes for coffin and burial fixtures."

(10-30-1891) "Funeral of Johnson baby. All the camp turned out. Al and wife were here for supper...."

Crystal River Current:
(10-1-1897) "Harry Gordon Howard, a resident of Crystal and miner, was taken ill by what he thought was a simple case of biliousness. Last week, the doctor was summoned to find Mr. Howard with fever which fast developed into typhoid. He died in his sleep."

Unplanned Dip...
(12-3-1897) "Yesterday our friend Joe Fisher had the misfortune to fall in the river near his tunnel. It is needless to say he used imported language for a while."

The Usher Family suffers illness and death…
(1-21-1898) Baby Alice Usher died of typhoid fever. She was buried in the Crystal Cemetery.

(1-28-1898)-"James Usher is on the sick list today, threatened with an attack of fever, which we hope will be checked."

(2-4-1898) *"Died;-Thursday, February 3, at ten o'clock a. m., the spirit of Neva Nettie, daughter of Mr. and Mrs. James Usher, departed from its earthly tenement, after a short sojourn of nine years, three months and sixteen days. She had contracted scarlet fever. She was buried in the Crystal Cemetery. Mr. C. Ambrose Williams conducted the service in the yard of the Usher house and then she was laid to rest. Friends sent beautiful flowers and they were woven into wreathes and garlands."*

Illnesses…
(2-11-1898) *"T. O'Bryan is under the weather with the grippe. George Young came down from Snow Mass Wednesday to recover from a severe cold."*

(3-25-1898) *"William Bermingham is suffering from a severe attack of neuralgia which has settled in his face."*

Explosion...
(5-20-1898) "An explosion occurred at the Crystal Mountain Mine last Tuesday, at 11:10 a.m., resulting in three men being injured. Doug Kellis was helping on the machine. He received injuries about the head and right arm. His eyes are badly burned and he may lose the sight of the right one. His little finger was also blown off just below the second joint on his right hand. Two other miners were slightly injured. The drill hitting an unexploded charge caused the explosion."

(6-17-1898) "Doug Kellis came down to camp yesterday for the first time since the explosion in the mine. He is improving rapidly and will soon be recovered. Little Helma Fortsch, age four, met Doug Kellis and said, 'I know you, you're Doug Kellis from the mine an' got blowed up and killed.'"

Fire...
(8-5-1898) "Wednesday afternoon, Geo W. Melton prevented what might have proved a destructive fire, by prompt action. The Swede's cabin caught fire from the flue at the roof and Mr. Melton happening to see the embryo conflagration, by taking up a few buckets of water to quench the flames, easily put it out."

Accident at the Sheep Mountain Power House...
(12-30-1898) "Tuesday afternoon, the first
accident resulting in serious injury ever to take
place at the power house of the Sheep Mountain
Tunnel, occurred and in consequence W. B.
Roddan is confined to his room bound up in
surgeon's bandages. Tuesday morning the
penstock was opened and the wheels set in motion.
The great compressor pumps filled the receiver;
both at the powerhouse and the mines, and at the
Bear Mountain Mine the machine men with the
assistance of the blacksmith were repairing a
break when the accident took place. As the
machine was idle, the gauge on the compressor
moved around until a head of one hundred pounds
was indicated, and pumping against this pressure
the wheels revolved more slowly. The engineer
applied soap to the big drive belt, holding the bar
in his left hand. He was standing near the drive-
wheel and in an instant the belt had caught the
clothing and drawn his arm into the pulley. With
his knee against the frame, he succeeded in
stopping the belt, which was only possible because
of the heavy backpressure from the receivers.
With his disengaged right hand he reached for a
penknife, and when about to remove it from his
pocket it dropped back. The sudden motion of
grasping the knife caused his knee to slip and the
belt, like a ravenous monster, pulled him farther
in, until the left shoulder was under the wheel.
Again bracing himself, this time with his head and

shoulders, he succeeded in holding the fearful odds of natural force pitted against human strength, determination and reason. This time the knife blade opened and reaching around his body, he cut the sixteen-inch belt, first from one edge then the other, until at last it was severed and he dropped to the floor, bruised and bleeding and almost exhausted. Again reason asserted itself, and realizing that he must have assistance, he groped his way to the door, where the crisp air revived him, and he staggered across the bridges where Mrs. Horace H. Williams ran to his assistance. With the help of the lady, he walked to his home, and five minutes later the reaction came with attendant suffering. Mrs. Geo. H. Tays was summoned and her skilled aid did much to relieve the pain while awaiting the surgeon's arrival. Surgical aid was called from Marble, Dr. Fuller reaching Crystal about noon. Examination revealed that no bones were broken; the muscles of the left arm and shoulder were torn and the ligaments parted from the bones; the body was bruised over the heart and lungs and the face cut and bruised. Though the injuries are not considered dangerous, Mr. Rodden will suffer a great deal of pain and it will be some time before his left arm will be strong again. He is getting along splendidly and the attending surgeon does not anticipate serious results. All of Crystal, where people are very much as members of one big family, rejoices that the injuries sustained were not more serious. Mr. Roddan is one of our best citizens and had but recently taken the position of engineer at the powerhouse. His rare presence of mind in the midst of great danger commands warm admiration."

Illness…
(1-13-1899) "The Inez, owing to the grippe epidemic, is compelled to suspend operations until Monday the twenty-third."

(1-13-1899) "Baby Allen Wright was sick Wednesday with prevalent contagion, but was much better again yesterday."

Accident at Crystal Mountain Eating House…
(2-17-1899) "Tuesday, Mrs. V. A. Cobb, suffered a painful injury, cutting a deep gash in her right forearm. In passing the front door of the eating house, hurriedly and thinking the door stood ajar, when it had been closed; her arm struck the glass panel, shattered the plate and was caught on the jagged edges of the glass and a deep cut inflicted. The wound was dressed by Mrs. Tays, and is healing as rapidly as could be expected."

Tin Poisoning…
(3-10-1899) "Last Thursday, Clyde Fulton was seized with cramps and suffered fearful agony for two days, suffering to all appearances of tin poisoning, resulting from eating canned tomatoes.

We are glad to announce that he is able to be up and around again."

Sled Accident...
(4-28-1899) Melton was bringing a hand sled of wood down a hill. He lost control, and the right side of his face was severely bruised on a tree while the passing logs on the sled tore the left side of his face. He had to have several stitches and peeked out of bandages until he was healed.

The Dark Angel...
(5-12-1899) Three-year-old Jimmy Baroni, eldest son of Mr. and Mrs. John Baroni, died of pneumonia. Because the family was Catholic and there was no priest available the family did not hold a funeral service. The body was laid to rest near the Crystal Cemetery.

Chicken-Pox...
(5-12-1899) *"Miss Aldean Roddan was ill with chicken-pox last week. She is doing much better."*

Burned...
(5-19-1899) *"Sunday morning Master Clyde Eugene Fitch learned a severe lesson. Being only a little more than one year old, he was toddling around the room and placed his two pink palms against the hot stove and before his mamma could rescue him, the little fellow's hands were one mass of blisters. The burns did not prove deep and after*

the first couple of hours, he seemed to suffer very little. Master Clyde has shown great fortitude in his sufferings, and we are pleased to note the injuries will soon be healed."

Horse Throws Rider...
(6-9-1899) "Monday afternoon James Arthur met with an accident which caused him much suffering. Riding down the canon alone, he was thrown from his horse. He was thrown upon his side, and the arm and side were so bruised as to render him helpless and he was found by James Usher, who placed him on a horse and brought him to Crystal, where he has since been confined to his bed at the home of C. M. Hiatt."

The Dentist Pays a Visit...
(7-14-1899) "Dr. Miller, the dentist, arrived in camp Tuesday evening and has had a great amount of work to do since."

Successful Operation...
(7-14-1899) "Dr. Melton performed a surgical operation for Horace H. Williams, Monday, removing a tumor from the forehead just in front of the left temple. The operation was entirely successful and no scar will result."

The Dark Angel...

(8-4-1899) "Died; Saturday morning, July 31st, at five o'clock, the spirit of Ole Carlson departed its earthly tenement. Several months ago he contracted a cold, which developed pleurisy and then pneumonia with symptoms of typhoid, and despite all that could be done, death resulted. He was a giant of a man, 52 years of age, from Throndhjem, Norway. Services were held at the Crystal Cemetery at 4 o'clock Sunday afternoon."

Mountain Fever...
(8-11-1899) "Mrs. V. A. Cobb has been numbered among the sick this week. She has been threatened with mountain fever but is able to be out again."

Services Offered to the Citizens of Crystal . . .

Communications...

The *Crystal River Current* (yearly subscription of $3.00) and later *The Silver Lance* (yearly subscription of $2.50) provided the town with the latest news. The newspapers were published once a week and were available on Saturday. The *Silver Lance* newspaper merged with the *Marble City Times* newspaper in 1899.

The Crystal Post Office had mail delivered by stagecoach on a daily basis when the road was not blocked. In the winter, depending on snow slides and weather, the mail was picked up and delivered by snowshoe (skis) to Crystal on Tuesday, Thursday, and Saturday.

A telegraph line went from Marble through Crystal and continued on to Crested Butte. A telephone line was installed from Marble to Crystal in 1904. In 1905 the Black Queen Mine and Mill were connected to the telephone line.

Drinking Water...

The water was supplied from a spring, which flowed down a hand-dug ditch to the town. This water was very good and safe to drink in the spring; but after the various animals had made their deposits in the open ditches, typhoid was a definite possibility. The ditch branched at the eastern end of town, allowing water to flow on each side of the street.

(8-12-1898) "H. R. Maurer has proved himself fully entitled to a seat in the city council; he cleaned out the water ditch on the north side of the street yesterday."

Schooling...

The one room Crystal School, which still stands today, was built of six by twelve inch

70

timbers laid edgewise, one on top of the other. Then one by six inch rough furring strips were nailed vertically every two feet. The outside was covered with shiplap siding, and the inside was completely covered with pine-beaded ceiling. It was typical construction in a new country where lumber was plentiful and cheap. In 1900, six-year-old John Williams carved his initials (J W) in the north side of the school. This can still be seen today (his "J" was made backwards). John Williams attended this school through eighth grade.

The following are school related articles from the local newspapers and the *Edgerton Journal:*

(5-4-1891) "Melton, Fish, Wright, Baley, Burnett and I went to Gothic to attend a school meeting to try to get a school started in Crystal."

(5-26-1891) The Edgerton Journal reported, "Worked on school house- Fish, Tays and I."

This is the first record of the building of the school house. The journal mentions many days when work was done on the school house until its completion on June 7, 1891. Among those given credit for their work on the school were Fish, Tays, Lyons, Whitbeck, Frank Williams, Burmingham, Charles Melton, O'Flanigan, and Frank Edgerton.

(6-10-1891) Edgerton Journal… "Last night had local school meeting in evening and I agreed to go to school election on Saturday the 13th."

(6-13-1891) Edgerton Journal… "School Election at Gothic today and every one is going. Twenty-four did go and we elected A. B. Fish for treasurer by 25 majority vote. Mrs. Melton Brownell & Burnette went. That's never for ladies. It's twelve miles to the school election & over 10 feet of snow part of the way…"

(9-4-1891) "Miss Enwall became the first teacher in the Crystal School."

(6-1-1893) Edgerton Journal… "Miss Dora Cochran arrived in Crystal from the east to teach at the Crystal School."

(7-12-1893) Edgerton Journal… "Received School Dictionary."

(6-23-1894) Edgerton Journal… "Miss Smeltzer arrived in Crystal to teach the school."

(7-6-1894) Edgerton Journal… "Organ placed in Crystal Schoolhouse."

(7-19-1894) Edgerton Journal… "Miss Smeltzer

is teaching school in the Cline house. The school house is undergoing many improvements which will add to its beauty and comfort."

(12-3-1897) "Miss Gladys Melton is conducting a winter school for the children of the camp"

Miss Dora Cochran, Teacher   Edward Melton Fortsch collection

(5-6-1898) "Miss Ida Freeman in Crystal on Saturday last from Carbondale to take charge of the school at this place for the ensuing term."

(7-22-1898) "We understand that a library is to be put in at each of the schools in this district. Nothing contributes more to the welfare of a school or community than a circulating library, and with the nucleus already at the Crystal school the addition of a few more volumes will make a most creditable library."

(7-22-1898) "Miss Mary E. Wallace, County Superintendent of Public Instruction, was a Crystal visitor Monday and Tuesday, on her tour of inspection of county schools and expressed herself well pleased with the manner in which Crystal school is advancing."

(2-10-1899) "SCHOOL REPORT–FOR THE MONTH OF JANUARY- Number of pupils enrolled seven: Flo Roddan, Don Roddan, Albert Usher, Elva Ward, Lela Ward, Rosie Rosetti, and Jimmie Rosetti. Number of pupils absent one. Number of pupils tardy none. Deportment of each pupil for the month 100. Lela Ward was absent one day on account of sickness. The promptness of the children in attendance is to be commended, not one having been tardy up to this time. J. L. Winters, Teacher."

(3-10-1899) "There will be a teacher's examination held next Thursday and Friday by the county superintendents of the State."

(3-17-1899) "Today is the last day of the winter term of school and this afternoon at two o'clock the school will entertain the public with a short literary program."

(3-30-1899) "The children are enjoying their spring vacation immensely."

(4-14-1899) "Miss Ida Freeman the teacher for the spring term of school reached camp Sunday. We are glad to welcome her back."

(4-14-1899) "The spring term of school opened Monday morning."

(4-28-1899) "Monday the annual school election will be held at Crystal for the election of a President and Secretary of the board of education of this district, to succeed Leonard Hoffman and C. A. Williams the present incumbents of the respective offices. The president will be elected for a term of three years, and the Secretary to fill an unexpired term of two years."

(5-5-1899) "The School election was a very quiet, Monday, and only twenty-six votes were polled. N. W. Ward was chosen president of the board for a full term of three years, and C. A. Williams was elected secretary for a two-year term. Each received a unanimous vote."

(5-12-1899) "The first month of the spring term of school was completed last week, with teacher and pupils well pleased with the progress made."

(6-9-1899) "School began last month with an attendance of eight. Those neither absent nor tardy during the month were Flora Roddan, Don Roddan and Vera Finley. There being a total absence of two days, both of which were caused by illness, and three tardy marks. Ida M. Freeman."

(6-16-1899) "Miss Mary E. Williams, County Superintendent of Public Instruction, came in on Tuesday's stage and visited the Crystal school Wednesday and the Marble school yesterday."

(6-30-1899) "Today the spring term of the Crystal school closed after a very satisfactory three month's work. There are larger schools than this, but none nicer anywhere. The pupils rendered a splendid program this afternoon, which was as follows:

"SummerAlphabet"..............................School
Song, "Come Away,"............................ School
Rec. "Children's Flower's,"...................Flo Roddan
Rec. "The Census,"............................. James Rosetti
Rec. "I'm Only a Penny,".....................Lella Ward
Song, "Summer Time,"..........................School
Rec. "A Little Boys Trials,"................... Albert Usher
Rec. "The Sweetest Place,".....................Vera Finley
Solo, "Down on the Ohio,".....................Flo Roddan
Rec. "Talking to Dolly,".......................Rosa Rosetti
Rec. "The Dandelion,"..........................Don Roddan

Song, "If I Have a Lesson,"………………. School
Rec. "Kitty,"……………………………Ezra Hiatt
Rec "A Naughty Little Girls Views of Life,"Flo Roddan
Rec. "Letting the Old Cat Die,"……………Elva Ward
Song, "Good-bye,"…………………………. School

Don Roddan was awarded a prize of a handsome pen for superiority in language work.

Miss Freeman treated the pupils to a liberal supply of candy and nuts and the pupils generously divided with visitors.

The school board held a meeting this forenoon, at which it was decided to retain the present teachers at both Marble and Crystal at the same salary as at present, the next fiscal year's school to be a term of nine months which is to begin August 28th. Miss Freeman has signed the contract to teach the Crystal school."

(9-29-1899) "The first month of the Crystal school opened with an attendance of nine and closed last Friday with an enrollment of fourteen."

Sunday School…

By 1900 Crystal began to offer a Sunday School for the children. Since there was no church building, the Sunday School was held in the schoolhouse on Sunday afternoons. Leonard S. Rohrer was the first superintendent of the Sunday School.

Weather and Road Conditions...

(4-26-1892) Edgerton Journal...
"Stormed some all day and wind is the worst I ever saw in Crystal. It unroofed Jim Ushers house and blew down lots of timber."

(4-8-1898) "Weather at Crystal the past month has been a remarkable mixture of spring and winter. Brilliant sunshine has been alternately mixed with snow, chilly nights, and wind in a way to puzzle the weather profits[sic], as they never were before. But just at present the weather clerk is doing all right if he does not change his mind again."

(5-26-1898) "On and after May 20th, the stage fare between Crystal and Redstone will be $2.50; Marble to Redstone, $1.75. With privilege of hand baggage.-C. M. Hiatt."

(12-23-1898) "Oliver Thomas and his drivers did quite a bit of work on the Lizard Lake hill as they came up Sunday afternoon, and it is now in fair condition."

(12-30-1898) "Yesterday morning a snow storm set in which has all the appearance of being a prelude to heavy snows peculiar to this section of the mountains."

(12-30-1898) "Wednesday the music of the snow slides came down from the Sheep Mountain cliffs."

(2-3-1899) "The dull, heavy roar of snow slides has been heard frequently this week."

(2-3-1899) "Wednesday the water was so low in the flumes that the compressor could not furnish air for the drills."

(2-3-1899) "This week the stage line commenced bringing two drivers through every day as a guard against accidents in coming through the canon."

(2-3-1899) "It is conceded this winter will not have a snow fall as great as when it was possible to snow-shoe from the top of Mineral Point to the top of Sheep Mountain- which was probably in the Glacial Period of geologic history."

(2-10-1899) "To all appearances this is going to be a winter remarkable for the number of snow slides."

(2-10-1899) "Wednesday night the storm settled down to a steady snow-fall and more than a foot of snow came down in twelve hours."

(2-10-1899) "Sunday night was the coldest of the season, the thermometer registering twenty below

zero at six o'clock Monday morning. Tuesday night was not a hot one either, but the mercury was up to twelve degrees."

(2-17-1899) "Last Saturday the citizens of Crystal turned out to help open the road through the canon which had been traveled part way by a team drawing a sled loaded with freight from Marble the day before. About thirty-five persons all told turned out and by evening had succeeded in opening a trail through to camp, though the original intention of opening the stage road was abandoned, when the extent of the snow over the track was realized in full."

(3-10-1899) "Hiatt says he wants to open up the road so as to bring the sled in again."

(3-10-1899) "By actual measurement the snow slide at the cemetery is 227 yards."

(3-17-1899) "The weather this week is of the variegated sort with a generous stock of snow arriving in daily installments."

(3-17-1899) "The lower bridge is still in danger of breaking down. In view of the fact that the people of Crystal and Marble have built four bridges there without expenses to the county it seems it might be economy[sic] to shovel the snow off, rather than build a new bridge."

(3-31-1899) "N. W. Ward has shoveled the snow from in front of his windows, much to his own delight."

(3-31-1899) "MARCH WEATHER A MATTER OF RECORD: 'But Old Sol came out to bid the month a bright adieu, and now comes April's many moods.' A week ago we were confidently looking for the bleating of the closing era of the month. It will be remembered by Lance readers that at Crystal March came in with a ferocious roar that, if the old tradition holds would portend a mild close. But this was none of your pet Mons, to be led with a dog chain when out for a Sunday afternoon constitutional. It has shown itself a veritable 'Prince of the Jungle' (with apologies to the Black Cat) and has outstripped records of bygone days in a degree that has outdone all predictions of old timers.

The few bright days only served to awake empty expectations of springtime's balmy breezes and soft sunshine, to be shattered by the new snowdrifts before the dining room window next morning.

Friday was rather a bright day, but Saturday brought heavy wet snow and rain and lowering clouds. Sunday morning a heavy blanket of new snow laid over the landscape. From nine inches to a foot was the depth measured in different places about camp, while at the Burt and at Crystal Mountain it was from twenty inches to three feet.

About seven o'clock the snow slides began breaking from the cliffs and gulch's[sic] and for several hours the deafening crash of snapping timbers and grating boulders was heard every little while. A slide came down the gulch between Bear and Little Bear Mountains which spread out in the valley of Crystal River canon upon an area full six hundred feet square. A party of gentlemen who visited this slide Monday morning made calculations as to the magnitude of the mass, which will give a reader some conception of it: The pile is reckoned to contain about two hundred thousand cubic yards of snow which is almost as compact as ice, and therefore represents from seventy-five to one hundred and twenty-five thousand tons of weight, or more than the tonnage of all our first-class battleships. A more readily conceived illustration is that if loaded upon 33-foot standard-gauge freight cars, with an engine to each train of twenty cars would make a solid line thirty-five miles long. If this line of trains were to be run on a schedule of twenty miles an hour, and held ten minutes apart, they would extend for a distance so great that the engine of the first train would be whistling for the Cypress yards at Kansas City when the last section leaves Crystal.

At the Burt the slides commenced to run Saturday, and one coming down the gulch blocked the mouth of the middle tunnel, where the men were working and it took them three hours to dig out. As a matter of precaution work was closed down at the Burt until the weather is more settled.

The Crystal Mountain Mine also closed down to avoid danger to employees and will not resume until the slides have run which may be within a few days and may not be for ten days.

Chicago Basin slide came down early Sunday morning, and Black Eagle gulch contributed its portion that afternoon. A new slide struck the lower bridge and it is probably broken down, while the Whitehouse St. Louis Basin slide came over and between the two bridges and buried the road between the bridges for the first time this year.

It is estimated that the slides coming down Bear Creek gulch have filled the gulch for over 150 yards to a depth of thirty feet, being filled to the level of the boarding house of the Crystal Mountain Mine.

At Snow Mass there is between seven and eight feet of snow.

Up along Crystal canon above the Belle head gate, along where great cliffs frown upon the narrow canon below, there must be acres of ice, cast from the dizzy heights in avalanches.

But today, the last of the month, as if to verify the old superstition, the day is warm and bright."

(4-7-1899) "The stage line is now using a stage, sled and pack-horse to convey the mail and passengers from Redstone to Crystal."

(4-14-1899) "The snow is getting so soft that Stage Driver Hiatt was compelled to leave his horse about half way between here and Marble when he came up Wednesday."

(4-21-1899) "The county commissioners have realized the need of the change in the road at Lizard Lake hill and have kindly contributed $250 to aid in the change."

(5-19-1899) "H. R. Maurer had the distinction to be a passenger on the first stage, Monday, returning from his Glenwood trip. The last sled of the winter went out of Crystal the morning of Feb. 1st."

(5-19-1899) "The Denver & Rio Grand offers a rate of one fare for the round trip, $1.75, from Carbondale and Aspen for Decoration Day."

Crops, Hunting, Fishing, and Sighting Game . . .

The *Edgerton Journal* reported the following crops grown in Crystal in the spring of 1893: raspberries, plum trees, currant bushes, grape vines, seed potatoes, carrots, cabbage, lettuce, beets, tomatoes, radishes, and green beans. Crystalites would go to Scofield in September to pick currants.

(8-27-1887) "Fishing has been extraordinarily good down the river of late. Charlie Melton and Bill Wood caught upwards of ninety, one day this week which weighed from half a pound to four pounds each."

(11-11-1897) "There is an abundance of small game in the vicinity of Scofield. Fox, wolves, lynx, porcupine, and skunks abound."

(7-2-1897) "Several trout were caught down stream, weighing 4 pounds."

(7-23-1897) "A bear knocked the senses out of a dog the other day which sent him crazy, and the animal, which was considered valuable, was obliged to be killed by its owner."

(7-23-1897) "Bill Sleeman captured a coyote pup a couple of weeks ago, but the little fellow begged so hard to be free that he is once more roaming at will in the haunts of his family."

(7-30-1897) "Bill Sleeman's coyote left the mark of its teeth on his hand. That was really the reason he turned it loose."

(9-24-1897) "A 585 lb. bear was killed at Marble and the people down there have been feasting on the 'fat of the land'. "

(6-3-1898) "Too bad this is the closed season: grouse are reported more plentiful than usual on Sheep Mountain and Mineral Point."

(6-3-1898) "Mrs. Dennis and Mrs. May while out walking one afternoon last week, report having seen a bear, near the Belle head-gate."

(2-10-1899) "The boys at the Burt have been having some sport of late, trapping for the wild animals which have been prowling around the store house. Their efforts have been rewarded by the capture of a fine specimen of lynx and a red fox and expect to add a lion and a wild cat to the collection soon."

(2-10-1899) "A very large eagle was seen last Tuesday flying along the cliffs of Sheep Mountain.

He alighted on a tree just back of Jack Wise's house. After remaining several minutes viewing the situation he spread his pinions and sailed away up Snow Mass canon. Mrs. Wise has a number of interesting pensioners in the birds of the neighborhood, which gather around her door for the food she always has ready for them. Several of them are quite tame while the antics of the saucy blue jays, 'camp-robbers' and woodpeckers are a source of constant amusement and interest."

(6-16-1899) "It is reported that the game wardens are taking special precautions to catch violators of the game laws in Gunnison and Pitkin counties, especially in the matter of protecting grouse, which at the nesting season are very tame."

(7-7-1899) "Geo. C. Eaton, Y. B. Ford, V. A. Cobb, George Henneforth and Robert Eaton spent Monday hunting wild game on Snow Mass. Two porcupines were the sole reward."

(7-14-1899) "H. R. Maurer and C. B. Lofton had the good fortune to feast their eyes on two handsome elk, on the north slope of Meadow Mountain."

(7-21-1899) "Open seasons are beginning; it is time for doves to be hiding."

(9-1-1899) "The Melton fishing party...landed 140 trout, and had a royal time. Mrs. Melton fished for wild ducklings with poor success, and many other incidents of interest were hinted at in the story of the outing."

Other Interesting Articles...

(5-21-1887) **Frank Edgerton reported in his journal,** *"A bath house was erected over a hot springs near Crystal. Took a bath in the Crystal Hot Spring."*

(7-09-1891) **Frank Edgerton wrote in his journal,** *"Mrs. A. B. Fish had twins, a boy and a girl."*

(6-07-1892) **Rose Edgerton reported,** *"Mrs. Burnet is the mother of a bouncing boy weighing eight and one-half pounds."*

(9-9-1893) **The** *Edgerton Journal* **reported,** *"A band of Gipsies [sic] on their way to Gothic. There were five teams of Gipsies [sic]."*

(8-12-1898) "Sunday evening an eight foot edition of Old Glory was raised to the top of a flagstaff over the Colorado Trading Company's Store. The staff is 22 feet above the top of the building, and is the product of H. R. Maurer's and E. E. Fitch's skill."

(4-14-1899) "Judge O'Bryan's cat got the idea that it was a fighter but met its match and the consequences is[sic] it crawled into a sack containing a large rock and fell into the river below the dam."

(5-5-1899) "Wednesday morning Charley Wilson and John Anderson had a whole lot of sport; they put up a target in the Swede cabin and had target practice for an hour or two."

(6-16-1899) "George H. Tays has been rather busier than usual this week and can give some valuable pointers on how to clean house and how to put blue denam[sic] on the wall."

(10-20-1899) "Tuesday the election judges met as the board of registration. According to the registration over seventy votes should be cast at Crystal."

(9-1-1899) "A Crystal young man acted very foolishly Tuesday night, and recklessly discharged fire-arms in close proximity to the heads of persons whom he chose to wake up at unreasonable hours. Wednesday he ran against the new city organization at Marble and contributed to the treasury of that town. We hope he is ashamed of his folly by this time—he ought to be out of respect to his friends and relatives."

The Crystal newspapers did not mention drinking problems in town. However, Frank Edgerton wrote in his journal:

(9-21-1892) "Returned from Uzzells Bi Chloride of Gold Cure. Cured of drunkenness and am once again myself. Free from all desire to drink liquor & I here & now register a solumn [sic] vow that if I ever again touch it that it will be my own fault and I hope to God it will kill me instantly."

(12-3-1882) Edgerton wrote, "Melton and Thomas O'Bryan started for Denver to take the Gold Cure at Uzzell Institute. I armed them with a letter of introduction...bully for them. They will miss lots of drinks. But to hell with the drink. They will come home sober men and proud to say that they have taken the Gold Cure."

Uzzell's Noble Work Property of the Gold Institute was located in Denver and advertised in the Denver newspaper. It proclaimed that it would cure those having liquor and opium habits. The facility was operated by Rev. Tom Uzzell. Home cooked meals, cheerful surroundings, and reading material consisting of books, newspapers and periodicals were offered at the institute. Liquor was furnished until one's taste for it had entirely passed. *Edgerton's Journal* indicates that drinking was a problem in Crystal.

(5-24-1895) The Gunnison Tribune announced, "Upon a petition of various citizens of Crystal, the county clerk is instructed not to issue a permit to anyone for the sale of liquor at that place."

For all intents and purposes, the town of Crystal had become a ghost town by 1920. Transportation, accessibility, and the low price of silver ore proved to be the demise of this once thriving mining camp.

PART II
THE NEXT 50 YEARS

The People of Crystal . . .

The residents of Crystal during the past fifty years are listed in the appendix. The people who reside in Crystal prefer to keep it as is – a cool and peaceful relaxing haven. They are continually working to preserve and restore the remaining cabins.

Helen Collins and Dorothy Tidwell   Carolyn Lodge collection

New Business Ventures. . .

Crystal City Guide Service...

Richard (Dick) Car-Skaden, a teacher in Aspen, arrived in Crystal in 1954, driving a Model A that had two transmissions. Dick, a tall, thin man, had unruly hair and a beard and wore glasses. He was an avid hiker and loved the mountains. Dick resided in the back of the Crystal Club. He took tourists on hiking trips, using huskies as pack animals for the food and camping gear. Dick lost his leg below the knee in a hunting accident but continued to hike. Dick's delicious spaghetti sauce was well known in Crystal.

Richard Car-Skaden   **W. Joe Neal Cartoon**

"Sarge" Jackson's Horseback Trips…

Theodore (Sarge) Jackson, a retired army sergeant, brought his horses to Crystal in 1954 to take tourists and hunters on horseback trips into the mountains. He stayed in various cabins in Crystal and later took his horses to Schofield where he lived in a mining shack and from there operated his business. Sarge would often allow the residents of Crystal to ride his horses. C-Rations, Rubber Legs, and Silver were three of them. Sarge always rode C-Rations. One memorable experience of Sarge's generosity in allowing others to ride his horses was when I was fourteen years old. A friend and I rode C-Rations and Silver to Lake Geneva. Sarge specifically told us, "Do not run the horses." On the way back to Lead King Basin, we decided to have a race with the horses. We were neck and neck; but as we rounded a curve, I remembered there was a deep, narrow ravine ahead in the road. There was no time to slow the horses. When we reached the ravine, the horses jumped. My horse made it to the other side, but my friend, riding C-Rations, hit just below the top of the ravine, and tumbled head over heels. My friend, airborne, flew past me as I was still riding at a gallop. Luckily, my friend was not hurt, and C-Rations only had a skinned nose. Sarge never asked about C-Rations, and I never told him.

Sarge Jackson on Pack Trip   Roger Neal collection

Another experience occurred when Maxine Fowler, riding Rubber Legs, and I, riding Silver, were attempting to lasso C-Rations. As my lasso went past Silver's eye, he spooked and began to buck. I was thrown off and landed on my back between two rocks. My parents and Sarge were very worried that I might have a serious back injury, but after a few weeks I was back to normal.

During the summer of 1958 two friends, William (Willie) Robinson and Duane Fowler, were asked by Sarge to go on an overnight pack trip to Avalanche Lake. They took one packhorse and three saddled horses. On their return from the lake one of the horses refused to leave. Sarge told Willie to ride double on Duane's horse, Midnight. Sarge said, "Your horse will come back to camp when he's ready." As they rounded the mountain out of sight, the horse that was left behind whinnied. Midnight decided he wanted to go back and tried to turn around on the narrow trail. As he turned, his back feet slipped off the trail, and he started falling backwards. Sensing the danger, Willie pushed Duane off the horse as it started tumbling head over heels down the side of the mountain. Halfway down Willie heard the horse's neck snap; and he came out of the saddle, landing in a small creek. It was only about forty or fifty feet but was very steep. Duane landed unhurt in a stream of icy-cold water. Although Willie survived, the little finger on his left hand was cut and was hanging by a piece of skin. It had begun to rain and was getting dark, so Sarge decided to camp for the night. Luckily, they were able to get a fire started by using Duane's damp matches. They wrapped Willie's finger and spent the night trying to stay warm by the fire. The next morning Sarge and Duane rode into Crystal and told us what had happened. Willie was walking down because he was in too much pain to ride a horse. My parents took Willie to a doctor in

Glenwood Springs where they were able to save the finger.

Perhaps Sarge shouldn't have been so willing to let others ride his horses.

Uranium Mining at the Inez...

In the summer of 1955 Bob Earhart and two other geologists from Ohio State University arrived in Crystal prospecting for uranium. The geologists were using Geiger counters and scintillation counters to detect the uranium. Bob Earhart and my father, Joe Neal, were using a scintillation counter on the Inez silver mine dump, when a deer fly bit my father's hand. He smacked the fly; and the counter needle moved to the right, causing it to make a loud ticking noise, which usually indicates the presence of uranium. My father thought he had broken the counter when he hit the fly. Bob then pointed his counter in the same direction my father had. His counter also reacted the same way. This ore had to come from the Inez mine during the silver mining days. Getting into the mine wasn't easy. The water had to be drained before they could enter the 1,500 feet of old tunnels. Beavers had made a twelve foot wide dam in front of the mine entrance. Ditching dynamite was used to blow up the beaver dam. This procedure allowed most of the water to drain from the mine. We then took Coleman lanterns and waded knee deep through the icy cold water. As we walked back into the mine we used Geiger and scintillation counters, trying to detect uranium in the mine walls. I was concerned about the beavers as they swam back and forth past my legs. About forty feet into the mine, we were out of the water. When we came to a branch in the tunnel, we took the left branch another forty feet and found a wall covered with uranium. This was the beginning of our mining adventure. My dad, relatives, and Kenneth Agee, an attorney from Columbus, Ohio, who sponsored the geologists, all helped to finance this adventure. The Midwest Exploration Company was formed.

The water was completely drained, and the ore cart tracks were restored. An air compressor was leased, and drilling equipment was secured. Dynamite fuses and caps were purchased. We used Carbide lamps attached to miners' helmets for light and head protection. We hired four miners. I was fourteen years old at the time and very gullible. The miners would say to me, "Roger, I bet you can't push the mining cart all the way into the mine." And "Roger, I bet you can't push that loaded mining cart all the way back out." Of course, I would say, "Yes, I can. I'll show you," and proceeded to push the cart all day long. After a day of this I wasn't so gullible.

One day, my dad, Dick Car-Skaden (one of the hired miners), and I were setting dynamite charges. Each of us had a pegboard with about twelve fuses. Each fuse was about six feet long (One foot equals one minute of burn time). All of the fuses were lit except one of Dick's. My dad went to help Dick with the fuse. He cut the fuse, split it, and attempted to light it with his Carbide light. All the fuses were now burning, except this one that he could not seem to get lit. After several cuts and splices he said, "Let's get the hell out of here!" As we ran out of the mine entrance the explosions started. As I turned and looked at my dad, he was smacking Dick in the head (really hard). Dust was flying in the air and I thought, "Boy, I'm glad I got all my fuses lit!" Then I realized what was really happening. Dick had taken his miner's helmet off and while holding his hat, he had scratched the back of his head. The Carbide flame had caught his hair on fire, and my dad was simply attempting to put out the fire. What I thought was dust was really smoke.

After three months of mining, we had three hundred pounds of uranium ore. We took it in our Jeep to have it assayed in Grand Junction. They informed us it was the highest grade ever found in the United States. We were very excited, thinking the ore had a value similar to gold. We told them we had three hundred pounds of ore in our Jeep. The assayer said, "When you have fifty tons, come on back." Needless to say, that was the end of our mining adventure. Like earlier mining adventures, a lot of work was done, but due to transportation and accessibility this mining adventure, too, came to an end.

The Starlight Campers...

During the summer of 1948 Bob Swanson (artist and pilot) and his friend Cal Heisler of Denver decided to embark in a business for tourists. They named their new business *The Starlight Campers.* They leased land near Crystal for the Starlight Campers' campground. A twenty-nine passenger custom-built air-conditioned bus, the Starlight Clipper, transported guests from Colorado Springs to Marble. Bob Swanson and his crew would bring horses from the Crystal campsite to Marble. When the guests arrived, they were given the choice of riding a horse or riding in the brand new jeep to Crystal. Most of the guests rode a horse. Once at the campsite the guests were wined and dined. A typical meal would consist of snow-chilled watermelon a la Colorado, grilled twelve inch Rocky Mountain rainbow trout with lemon butter or Blue Ribbon Colorado steaks, Indian corn on the cob, boot lace potatoes, forest loveapple salad, hot gypsy rolls, wild strawberry shortcake a la mode, woodsman's coffee or tea, and Colorado-fresh milk.

THE FIRST VISTA-DOME BUSS IN COLO.

Vista Dome Bus of Starlite Campers   Bob Swanson collection

Each guest was provided with an individual spick-and–span white tepee, feather-filled oversize sleeping bag (including fresh cotton sheets and linen covered pillows), full-length quilted air mattress, sparkling clean towels, sport and game necessities as required (horses, bow and arrows, boats, fishing license, rod, reel, flies, miner's pan and pick, etc.)-everything from a tent flashlight to a bar of soap and portable shower. This was a first class operation.

Starlite Campers in Crystal   Bob Swanson collection

Emmet Gould was the owner of the property leased by the Starlight Campers. Mr. Gould was considered the most colorful character Bob Swanson had ever met. The guests considered him a real man of the Old West, and he provided many stories around the campfires, telling of his mining days.

The Starlight Campers came to an end three years after it started. According to Bob Swanson, there were two reasons for its demise. First, Bob was recalled to active duty in the USAF because of the Korean conflict. Second, the Starlight Campers equipment was stolen from a storage building in Crystal. Bob Swanson is now retired and lives in Denver.

Treasure Mountain Ranch Corporation...
In 1938 Emmet S. Gould of Aspen came to Crystal. He was looking for ore to run through a recently purchased mill. He became interested at once in the area, not only for its potential mineral wealth but also for its wild beauty. He bought several mining claims, including the Old Mill and several city lots with their cabins. He made an effort to open the Lucky Boy and the Lead King mines, but with the outbreak of the war, it became impossible to get men and materials; and the effort failed.
The descendents of Emmet Gould have been coming to Crystal every summer since 1939. The relatives included Emmet's daughters, Helen (Gould) Collins and Dorothy (Gould) Tidwell. Helen had two daughters, Maxine and Carolyn. Carolyn remembers riding with boxes of dynamite in the back of her grandfather's truck. He told her if the dynamite blew up, she should peck the window to let him

103

know! These relatives and their descendents formed the Treasure Mountain Ranch Corporation in 1975. They have several summer cabins, which are still available for rent. The corporation also operates the Crystal Store. This store sells souvenirs, candy, and soda pop that is chilled by Rocky Mountain spring water.

Crystal Tale Books...
Since eight years of age I have been telling stories around the campfires to friends, family, and anyone interested in listening. I found that I had an audience ready to listen to my wildest stories. We would sit around the campfire at night, and I would tell stories about the area. There was just enough truth to make every story believable. A lot of my stories were entwined with my experiences of mountain climbing, working in mines, mountain rescues, and encounters with the wild life. *The Story of Little Blue Hound* is about a sheepherder, his dog, and their encounter with a bear. This story was developed when I was about nine years old. My parents allowed me to follow a sheepherder to his camp in the high country, and a new story was born. The story of *The Yum-Yum Ants* was created while I was splitting aspen logs for firewood. Big black carpenter ants came pouring out of a log. That and my experiences of mining in the Inez mine inspired a new story around the campfire. These children's

storybooks are available for purchase in Marble and Crystal.

Saving the Old Mill. . .

The Old Mill was built in 1893 and housed an air compressor that supplied air for drilling in the Sheep Mountain Tunnel. Operations of the mill were officially closed in 1917. Emmet Gould purchased the Old Mill, and it is now under the ownership of the Treasure Mountain Ranch. The owners are currently working with the Gunnison County Historical Society and the Aspen Historical Society for the preservation of this mill. Donations are accepted at the store in Crystal to assist with this effort. Many people have volunteered time, energy and money to assist with the preservation of the Old Mill. During the late 1950's Joe Neal became concerned about the possible collapse of the penstock. He attached cables to the rock foundation on the north side and secured the penstock by attaching to the rock on the south side. The Gunnison County Pioneer and Historical Society replaced the original roof in 1976. Albert and Conny Erhard constructed a foundation of rock and cement under the penstock for further stabilization.

In 1984 there was a record runoff that caused a four-inch split in the wooden structure.

The Old Mill   Bonnie Neal photo

The Aspen Historical Society spearheaded a drive for funds to stabilize the mill. In September of that year Richard Haberman engineered a system of cables and beams to repair the sagging porch of the mill. Wayne Brown and Oscar McCollum of Marble and Jack Roberts of Redstone assisted him.

Some Memorable Events. . .

A New Invention...

In 1949 Frank and Emily Reh were staying in one of the cabins in Crystal. I had been fishing; and as I walked past Emily's house, I noticed she was in her yard washing clothes. As I approached, I noticed she was using a wooden frame with a rough metal attachment. There was even a place to put a bar of soap on the frame. Emily would rub the soap and clothes back and forth on the rough metal. When I asked what she was doing, she replied, "I'm washing my clothes." I thought, "Wow, what a great invention!" I ran home and told my mother about Emily's new invention.

Water In Crystal...

During the first few years we lived in Crystal, the drinking, bathing, and laundry water came from the same hand dug ditch originally established by the Crystal founders. Every spring the sheepherders brought their sheep through the town of Crystal, and health concerns developed because of the water contamination. Joe Neal, a plumber, was put in charge of installing a plastic pipeline at the head of the Crystal Falls. The gravity fed water produced thirty-two pounds of water pressure. Joe then connected most of the houses to the water line. Later the line was extended to the spring's source which now measures 2,710 feet from beginning to end. As a result the water now has been tested and is actually more pure than some municipality water sources. Most of the cabins now have running water for kitchen sinks and bathrooms. Propane water heaters provide hot water.

Community Shower House...

Through the ingenuity of Joe Neal a shower house was constructed west of the Fogle cabin near the river. A water system was developed whereby a waterline was run to the shower house where a valve was installed on the neck of the showerhead. When this valve was closed and both the hot and cold water were turned on, water would run to a fifty gallon drum barrel that was on top of the hill above the shower house. When the barrel was full, the hot and cold water were turned off in the shower house. Then the shower valve was turned on, and a fire was built under the barrel to heat the water. When the water was hot, a person would have both hot and cold running water for a refreshing shower. Everyone enjoyed the use of the shower, but it was most appreciated by hiking groups after several days of hiking. This shower house has been disassembled since most of the cabins now have their own bath facilities.

Foot Injury...

In 1950 my family was staying in the cabin known as the Print Shop (originally The General Store). One night, as I walked barefoot, I stepped on a small piece of broken glass that became stuck in the bottom of my foot. I thought I had removed the glass from my foot; but as the days passed, my foot became very sore. When my mother asked me why I was limping, I told her there was a piece of glass in my foot. She looked at my foot and saw that it was quite swollen and red. My father said we had to get the glass out of my foot. He lit a Coleman lantern and had me lie on my stomach. My mother held me down while he probed with a needle to remove the glass. I was screaming and yelling at the top of my lungs. After what seemed like hours, but was probably just a few minutes, the glass was successfully removed. At times like this it would be great to have more accessible emergency care in Crystal.

Bombs Away!...

As a ten year old one of my favorite past times was to carry five gallon buckets and heavy wire to the Lucky Boy Mine. The Lucky Boy had a cable that ran approximately three hundred yards to the Crystal road. I would fill a bucket with rocks and dirt and fasten it to the cable. Given a slight nudge, it would start slowly but would soon travel at a high rate of speed to the bottom. The friction of the cable and wire usually caused the wire to break and the bucket to fall. One day a friend and I carefully placed cherry bombs into the sides of the five gallon bucket filled with dirt and rocks. We also used extra wire to fasten the bucket to the cable hoping it would make it to the bottom. We lit the fuses and pushed. Away it went down the cable, rocking back and forth as the cherry bombs exploded. At that time a Jeep tour from Swiss Valley Ranch appeared on the road. The people in the jeep probably thought they were being attacked when they saw the exploding bucket of dirt flying down the cable. The driver pushed the accelerator and sped away, not realizing there was no danger since the cable stopped about sixty feet from the road.

Crystallized Dynamite...

In 1955 my father found a bag of crystallized dynamite in a barn loft. He placed it in a hole and exploded it. I learned that after dynamite had been frozen, it could easily explode when dropped. That same year I found some crystallized dynamite. I put it in the water ditch, unwrapped it, and let it wash away. Luckily, it did not explode while I was handling it.

Run-Away Horses...

In the summer of 1955 Charlie Pascal brought two riding horses from Wade Loudermilk's corral in Marble to Crystal. Wade had given us permission to use the horses that day, but Charlie was expected to return them by six o'clock that evening. Charlie and I were going fishing at Love's Cabin which was located about three miles above Lead King Basin. When we reached Love's Cabin, we put the horses in the corral and went fishing. When we returned, we discovered the horses had broken the corral and had run away. Since it was getting late, we decided to spend the night and carry the saddles back to Crystal the next morning. The sheepherders used Love's Cabin so it was furnished with a cook stove, cooking supplies, and bedrolls. We spent most of the night telling stories and watching beavers work in the beaver ponds. We were walking in the wet grass, so my feet became very cold. The next morning we carried the saddles on poles across the river. As we waded across the icy cold water, my feet became extremely painful. I told Charlie I could not walk any farther. He built a fire to warm my feet. When I removed my shoes and socks, I discovered I had blisters, indicating my feet might be frostbitten. I sat by the fire warming my feet for about one half hour. Charlie suggested we put the saddles behind a boulder and come back later with horses to get them. After hiding the saddles, we began walking down the trail. About one half mile from Love's cabin we were surprised to see seven riders on horseback. Since the horses had returned to

Wade's corral in Marble without any riders, Wade thought something bad had happened to Charlie and me. They did not expect to find us laughing and joking about our ordeal. After being scolded because we had not returned that evening as expected, we led the search party to the saddles. As punishment we had to walk back to Crystal.

Today, Love's Cabin is still referred to as a destination, but the cabin has been destroyed by snow.

Road Experiences...

In 1956 I began driving our 1955 Jeep from Crystal to Marble. I would remove the canvas top, put the Jeep's windshield down, put on a leather bomber's helmet and goggles, and wrap a white scarf around my neck. My dad was in Indiana, and my mother in Crystal did not know that I was such a reckless teenage driver. I would fly down the road to Marble, trying to beat my best driving time of less than fifteen minutes. I would drive to Ken's Pop Stand to buy pop and peanuts from Theresa. As I flew through Marble, a cloud of dust arose when I slid around the corners. Residents of Marble started talking of getting a petition against my driving to town, so I began driving slower.

The road to Crystal   W. J. Neal Cartoon

My sister Patricia worked in Glenwood Springs at the Hotel Colorado. Sometimes I drove her to work from Crystal. Once we were late, and I was driving very fast in the open jeep. At that time the road from Marble to Carbondale was a dirt/gravel road. The Redstone Mid-Continent Coal Company was in operation, and huge coal trucks loaded with coal were traveling on the road to Carbondale. We were driving behind a coal truck for several miles; and by the time we arrived in Glenwood Springs, we were completely covered in dust. Needless to say, my sister had to take a shower before starting her job that day.

When it rains, mudslides on the road are always a concern. Lenny Cantor of Indianapolis, Indiana, learned quickly that his Toyota Land Cruiser was no match for a mudslide. He asked me to go with him to see a mudslide in progress. I rode down with him one half mile past the cemetery where the mud was flowing across the road. Lenny asked me if I thought his Toyota Land Cruiser could drive through the mud. I said, "No." Lenny said, "If I try it and get stuck, will you hook my winch to a tree on the other side?" I replied, "Sure." Lenny hopped into his Land Cruiser, backed a hundred yards from the slide, put the vehicle in four-wheel drive, and floored it. When he hit the center of the mud, the Land Cruiser quickly sank to its frame. Lenny was stuck! While standing on his seat, he yelled to me to tie the winch onto a tree. The mud was almost inside the open Toyota. I had difficulty getting to the vehicle because I was laughing so hard. After finally getting the winch tied to a tree, Lenny was pulled to safety. That same day a family from Kansas was sightseeing in Crystal. Due to the mudslide they were unable to leave. We invited them to eat with us and spend the night. The next day after the road was cleared, they were able to leave. This is often the case with travelers who are sightseeing in this remote area of Colorado. They are often forced to spend the night due to vehicle or road problems, and the people of Crystal are always very accommodating.

Bears...

Bears in the Crystal area include the brown, cinnamon, and black. These all belong to the black bear family. Over the years I have discovered that bears and snakes have a lot in common. Both can be very startling when they are met unexpectedly. Following are accounts of three bear stories that occurred around Crystal.

The first story occurred in the summer of 1953. The twin bridges had been destroyed two and one-half miles from Crystal and the only access into town was by foot. One day, two Texans strolled into town with pistols strapped to their legs. One looked about sixty years old and had a Colt .22 and a .45 in holsters. The other looked about forty years old and carried a .38. They were bragging about all the big game they had shot in different parts of the world. All during the day we could hear them shooting chipmunks and marmots. Early that evening, my brother and I were standing in front of the Crystal Club as the sun began to set on Crystal Peak. We heard two gunshots and saw the sixty-year-old man running toward us looking white as a sheet. He was stuttering, "I j-j-j-j-j-j-just sh-sh-sh-sh-sh-sh-shot a b-b-b-b-b-bear!" The three of us ran to our house and told my dad of the incident. The old man explained that he was climbing up a hill and saw a big brown rock near the top. As he approached the rock, the big brown rock stood up, and he realized it was a bear. He drew his .22 and began pulling the trigger, firing his last two cartridges. All of his .45 ammunition had been used on the chipmunks and marmots. My father lit the Coleman Lantern and the old man led us to the spot where he had shot the bear. There was blood all over the ground and a huge bear footprint that measured eight and one-half inches wide. One could see where the bear had fallen backwards, crushing the brush as it rolled down the hill into the river below. The two Texans stayed overnight in one of the cabins, and the next morning we heard their gunshots as they went down the valley. The following day as we walked down to our truck to go after supplies, we found a dead porcupine that had been used for target practice by the two fearless Texans. All during that summer I was concerned about a wounded bear attacking me while I was fishing.

In 1988 Duane and Dorothy Fowler spotted a bear on Bear Mountain across from the Crystal Cemetery. Everyone in town went down to see the bear. Carolyn Lodge was the first to see the bear. She kept telling me where the bear was, but I couldn't see it. She told me where to look and showed me how to shade my eyes from the sun by using my hands like binoculars. I told her that was silly; but after much prodding, I decided to try it. Carolyn said, "Look half way up the mountain where the stream is coming down. You will see a black bear, and he is moving a bush. He's probably eating berries." I looked at the exact spot and sure enough I could see much better with my "hand binoculars." A waterfall was hitting a bush that caused it to move, and the bear was a shadow from a tree. This incident resulted in the story of the "Grow Ho Bear," which I enjoy telling around the campfire, especially when Carolyn is present.

The third incident occurred in 1996. People had been reporting bear sightings all around the Crystal area. It seemed as if everyone, including first time tourists, had seen a bear, everyone that is, except me! I had never seen a bear during the fifty years I had been coming to Crystal. Every time someone saw a bear, I would grab my video camera and head for that location, only to be disappointed and to return without seeing the bear. One day Chris Cox informed me that he had seen a brown bear on the road near the Snow Bridge. I grabbed my video camera and started hiking up the road. As I neared the fork in the road to Lead King and Schofield, a bear suddenly jumped up and ran extremely fast up the hill to an aspen tree. It stopped, stood up, and holding onto the aspen tree, it looked down at me about twenty feet below. I wasn't s-s-s-s-scared. I was debating about whether to run down the hill and get out of there or to use my video camera. I decided no one would believe me if I didn't have proof, so I turned on the video camera, focused on the bear, and started video taping. Just to show everyone how brave I r-r-r-r-really was, I told the bear he better stay up there or I'd have to beat his butt. After taping for about one minute, I decided the bear might be getting hungry, so I turned off the record button, put the cap back on, and started running back to Crystal. Dail Lodge was on his front porch, so I ran over to show him the video. Excitedly I rewound the videotape and pushed the play button. The only thing on the tape was the video cap being put on the lens. After rewinding three times, I realized that in my excitement of finally seeing a bear, I had forgotten to push the record button. Later when I played it on a VCR after I put the cap back on, there was a black screen, but I could be heard running like crazy down the mountain.

Re-roofing the Crystal Club...
The Crystal Club was originally built in 1899. During the summer of 1992 Dail Lodge and I undertook the challenge of completely re-roofing the Crystal Club. This required the complete removal of the old shake shingles, boards, and rafters. The top log on the right side, which supported the rafters, had rotted and also had to be removed and replaced. We did not

have the availability of a crane for lifting the heavy twenty-four foot long spruce log. We were able to raise the log into position by laying four fifteen foot logs at an angle against the side of the building. Two cables ran from the top of the Crystal Club down under each end of the log and over the top of the Crystal Club where they were attached to two pickup trucks. As the trucks were driven slowly, the cables pulled the log, and the log rolled up the ramp to the top where it fell into a pre-notched destination. New rafters were built, new boards were put in place, and metal roofing was installed by use of power tools. A small gasoline generator was brought to the second floor of the Crystal Club for use with these tools. It was getting late in the day, and the sun was setting. We were very excited because our project was going to be completed that day. I was on top of the roof putting the last three screws in the last sheet of roofing when the generator ran out of gasoline. Dail went to the second floor to fill the generator with gasoline. Due to the lateness of the day it was very difficult to see because there was no light inside the room, and some gasoline was spilled over onto the spark plug. When Dail started the generator, it burst into flames. I asked Dail if he was having trouble because I heard him banging around. He replied, "There's a fire!" I yelled to my wife and Dail's daughter, Sharon, to get the fire extinguisher from our house next door. By the time I got down from the rooftop and reached the front door of the Crystal Club, Sharon had returned with the fire extinguisher. I took the extinguisher; and as we entered the Club, there was an orange glow in the back room. I knew then that the Crystal Club was going to be burned to the ground. Running to the back room, I met Dail pulling the generator down the stairs. The fuel tank was so hot that gasoline was spewing through the air holes and making a torch. Dail's shirtsleeve was also on fire. Pulling the trigger of the extinguisher, I sprayed Dail's arm and the generator. The fires were out, and the Crystal Club was saved. Dail had second degree burns on his arm, but he was the hero. If it hadn't been for him, the Crystal Club would have burned down. Due to his heroism and his concern for this historic building, he risked his life to save it.

There is a small residential area built onto the back of the Crystal Club. This provided housing accommodations for Dick Car-Skaden when he was living in Crystal during the 1950's. This was also a residence for John Toly, a local artist of the Crystal Valley, who is now residing in Carbondale. John lived in the back of the Crystal Club for several summers during the 1970's. His paintings show his affection for this area.

The Crystal Club Saloon   Bonnie Neal photo

Wedding Bells...

The following residents of Crystal chose to have their weddings in Crystal. In August 1991 Debbie Fowler and Steve Heise were married. In June 1998 Sharon Lodge and Dale Pitcher were married. Both couples chose the wooded area of aspen trees in the upper meadow as their wedding chapel. Here they said their vows as gentle breezes whispered through the trees. Each wedding was a special celebration, and this grandeur with its rich vegetation and natural beauty was the perfect location for these memorable events.

The Cabins of Crystal . . .

The Fogle Cabin...

In the summer of 1948 Welcome Joe Neal, a plumber from Indiana, with his wife, Esther Fogle and their three children, Patricia, David, and Roger, were camping in the Rocky Mountain National Park. While camping there, they met the Wittenborns from New York. The Wittenborns invited the Neals to go with them to Aspen to visit their friend Fritz Benedict. The Benedicts told their guests of a ghost town named Crystal and invited them on a picnic. Everyone agreed that this sounded like an exciting trip. Joe and his family had no idea that the road from Marble to Crystal would be extremely narrow. As Joe drove his pickup truck across the shelf road, he and his wife yelled to the kids in the back to stay on the left side of the truck. The tires on the right side were on the edge of the road, and rocks were falling to the river below. On the return trip to Marble the kids were ordered to the right side of the truck. The truck's fenders were scraped on the rocks as Joe cursed the road most of the way to and from Crystal. Although Joe vowed never to drive over that road again, the trip proved to be the turning point in the lives of the Neal family. They thought Crystal was one of the most beautiful places in the United States.

The Neal Family in Crystal, 1952   Neal collection
From left: Fogle, Roger, W. Joe,
Pat Miller, (family friend), David, Patricia

Joe and Fogle fell in love with Crystal, and every summer since 1948, they traveled to Crystal. Joe bought two mining claims, three cabins, and some lots in Crystal. Their roasted turkey and wine picnic turned out to be one of the best adventures they had ever taken. They lived in the first cabin on the left as one comes into Crystal from Marble. This cabin became known as the Fogle cabin and was originally built in 1892. It is thought to have been a store during the early days of Crystal and was originally constructed with a false front.

Fogle was able to enjoy spending her entire summer in Crystal. This was one of the busiest times for Joe's plumbing business in Mooresville, Indiana. He could not spend his entire summer but would make several trips back and forth to Crystal throughout the summer. When he came to Crystal, he spent a lot of time repairing roofs and siding, installing plumbing, working on foundations, etc. As a small child, I always wondered why he spent so much time working on the cabins. Now I know because I find I am doing the same things myself. Joe had also been a one time John Herron art student. He found, when he had the time, that Crystal was a perfect place to relax and paint.

Travelers were always welcome at the Neal's house in Crystal. People would often stop to ask questions about the area, receive help and assistance, or just spend time chatting. It was not uncommon for Fogle to invite strangers into her home. She was an exceptionally intelligent person and was able to engage people in discussions on any topic, especially politics. One day Fogle was sitting on her front porch when a vehicle stopped; and the man asked, "Is this the way to Schofield?" She said, "Yes, but you can't get there, because there's a snow slide across the road." The driver responded, somewhat perturbed, "Yes, I can; this vehicle has eight gears forward and two in reverse; and it can go anywhere." Fogle paused, smiled, and replied,

"Can it fly?" The driver drove away in a cloud of dust toward Schofield only to return a short time later driving past her without looking in her direction.

Another incident occurred when a driver stopped to ask for assistance. It seemed the axle had broken on his Scout. Fogle asked, "What year Scout is it?" After his reply she reached behind the kitchen door and pulled out an axle to fit that exact Scout. One can imagine the surprise of the owner to have found a much needed part in this remote ghost town of Crystal. Residents of Crystal seldom throw anything away. One just never knows, who might need what some people consider "a piece of junk."

Fogle Cabin   Bonnie Neal photo

Joe and Fogle are both deceased, but their descendents continue to spend their summers in Crystal. Mr. and Mrs. Kenneth E. (Patricia) Gray now reside in the Fogle cabin during the summer and fall. Their children, Jefferson Gray, and Douglas (Julie) Gray, spend as much time as they can in Crystal during their vacations.

The Erhard Cabin   Bonnie Neal photo

Erhard Cabin...
The small log cabin on the east side of Fogle's cabin is the Erhard cabin. Conny and Albert (Al) Erhard began coming to Crystal regularly in the 1950's. They were both well acquainted with living in the wilderness. Al was raised in Montana and worked in logging. They lived in Denver where Al was a chemical

engineer, and Conny was a teacher. They enjoyed coming to Crystal because of its remoteness and beauty. They became good friends with my parents, Joe and Fogle, and spent summer weekends camping and exploring the area. This was also an ideal place for their children, George and Eben, who also enjoyed the outdoors. Al was instrumental in working on the renovation of the Old Mill. Al's carpenter skills were put to good use, helping with the repair of the cabins and relocating the cabin next to the Fogle cabin. This cabin was originally built in 1890. The logs were beginning to rot, and the cabin was in desperate need of repair. The cabin was moved two lots east of its original location. A rock foundation was built, and the logs were reassembled and replaced with new as needed. A new floor was installed, and chinking was placed between the new logs. This became a new cabin for them to reside in while visiting Crystal. Al died in 1990, but Conny continues to spend as much of her summer as possible in Crystal.

The Hotel...

There is no original date of construction listed in the Gunnison County Courthouse for the hotel. The hotel was destroyed by fire and was completely rebuilt in 1977. The hotel is the residence of Dorothy Tidwell's descendents. Her grandson, Chris Cox, and his family come to Crystal every summer or fall.

The Dutchman   Bonnie Neal photo

The Dutchman...

This cabin was originally built in 1895 and is located between the Johnson house and the Hotel. It is owned by the Treasure Mountain Ranch Corporation and is one of their rental cabins.

The Johnson House...

This cabin was built in 1895 originally and is currently the residence for Carolyn and Dail Lodge. Carolyn and Dail spend their summers and falls living in Crystal. Dail, a doctor, and Carolyn, a nurse, have both been instrumental in assisting people during times of need. They often make 'house calls' for the residents of Crystal and assist with other emergencies. Their children and families, Dail, Jr., and Hannacho Lodge, Denver Lodge, and Sharon and Dale Pitcher, come to Crystal during their vacation times as often as possible.

The Johnson Cabin   Bonnie Neal photo

The Anderson House...

The Anderson house is the last two-story house at the east end of Main Street. It was originally built in 1889 by Rob Anderson's great-grandfather, George H. Tays, who lived there during the early days of Crystal. The house was sold to Charles and Gladys Bassett of Springfield, Illinois, in 1937. Mr. Bassett was a geology professor who came to Crystal with his wife to enjoy its beauty and serenity. Mrs. Bassett was considered a very "proper" lady and would often have formal dinners in their Crystal home for the various residents of Crystal. The

129

children of Crystal were often treated to an afternoon tea. In 1977 when the Bassetts decided to sell their Crystal home, they contacted Rob Anderson, who is a dentist in Glenwood Springs. Of course, he was delighted and jumped at the opportunity to purchase his great-grandfather's house. He and his wife, Manette, began a major remodeling effort in 1996. They and their children, Brynne, Tays, and Riley, spend much of the summer and fall of each year enjoying their Crystal cabin.

The Anderson House   Bonnie Neal photo

The Cinnamon Roll Meadow Cabin...

Bonnie and Leland Stanford from Oklahoma first came to Crystal with their Schnauzer dog, Sooner, in the summer of 1959. After Sooner died, they were given another Schnauzer puppy, and they named him "Show

Me," since they had now moved to Missouri. They built a cabin in the meadow near the old schoolhouse. This cabin and four others are connected for communication with hand cranked telephones. Bonnie is considered the official baker in Crystal, baking cinnamon rolls, pies, and other tasty delights on her Quick Meal wood stove. When my son, Joe was twelve in 1983, Bonnie offered to bake his birthday cake. When she asked him what kind of cake he would like, he replied, "chiffon." She was expecting a request for chocolate or something simpler and was somewhat surprised that a twelve-year-old child would request a chiffon cake. She wondered how she was ever going to make the cake on her wood stove at an altitude of 9,000 feet. But, of course, her promise held to bake the cake; and it was done to perfection. In June of 1998 Bonnie was asked to bake Granny Smith apple pies for the wedding of Sharon Lodge in Crystal. This was a very time consuming project to peel the dozens of apples, make the piecrusts, and bake them on the wood stove, which required hours of feeding the firebox to keep the oven hot. Bonnie delivered twelve beautifully baked pies. It is not unusual to see Bonnie walking down main street in Crystal, delivering a freshly baked pan of warm cinnamon rolls to some lucky recipient. One summer Bonnie decided to keep a record of the number of pans of rolls she baked. She made a total of 104 pans of cinnamon rolls that summer!

Bonnie and Leland are very interesting characters and are well known for their many true campfire stories. One of the best "Bonnie and Leland stories" in Crystal occurred when they were getting ready to retire one evening. This required a visit to the outhouse. After making a quick trip and returning to their cabin, they were surprised to find the front door had locked when they shut it. Now Bonnie was in a thin nightgown, and Leland was wearing only his jockey shorts and cowboy boots. They knew the Lodges had a spare key to their cabin, so they decided to walk over the hill to the Lodges' house on Main Street. Upon arriving, Bonnie was elected to go to the front door and ask for the key. Carolyn Lodge was a bit surprised to find Bonnie at her front door in just a nightgown. Bonnie had to explain what had happened; and when asked where Leland was, she told Carolyn he was standing over in the shadows. Carolyn shined her flashlight over and saw Leland. He said, "Don't shine your light over here!" Carolyn told Bonnie, "I don't have your key here, but I'm sure it's at Dorothy's house; I'll just call her." She immediately called Dorothy and asked if she had film in her camera and if she would bring it. After much consternation Leland agreed to let Carolyn take his picture with Bonnie so he could get the key and go home. No one knows where this picture is, but there are reports that it can still be viewed for a price.

At the age of eighty Leland purchased an ATV. The following poem was written in honor of his eightieth birthday:

Listen my friend and I'll tell you a tale
About a man named Leland, I knew him well.
He turned eighty on July 17th
And rode his four-wheeler that day, at length.
His wife, Bonnie, hanging on behind
Holding on to Show Me, as down the road they did wind.
They passed the Andersons, all amazed
That anyone eighty would be so crazed.
Leland flew by with a smile on his face
But Bonnie looked scared, like he was in a race.
Leland tore past the print shop, wastin' no time
As Dorothy, Carolyn and Dail heard
the four-wheeler whine.
Next came the Neals, but Roger was ready
An extension ladder would slow this Fast Freddy.
Leland had heard of this trick before
So he kicked it in high, and over the ladder
they did soar.
And with a laugh and a scream of delight
They rode the four-wheeler the rest of the night.
So be like Leland and enjoy your life
But first find a woman like Bonnie to be
your wife.
                                    Roger A. Neal

133

We were saddened by the death of Leland in July 2000. Bonnie continues to enjoy Crystal in the summers.

The Sperry Cabin...
This is the last original cabin on the right at the end of Main Street. This cabin was originally built in 1899. It is owned by the Treasure Mountain Ranch Corporation and is one of their rental cabins.

The Sperry Cabin   **Bonnie Neal photo**

The Brooks Cabin...

This cabin was originally built in 1899 and was the home of Maxine and Warren Fowler's family during the 1950's and 1960's. Maxine and Warren are deceased, but their children and families still continue to come to Crystal.

The Brooks Cabin   Bonnie Neal photo

The Print Shop...

This cabin, built in 1885, was the A. A. Johnson Store. It was the location for the printing of *The Crystal River Current* and *The Silver Lance* newspapers. The side building is the location for the current Crystal Store. The residential portion of the cabin is one of the Treasure Mountain Ranch Corporation rental cabins.

The Print Shop and Crystal Store   Bonnie Neal photo

The Crystal Store...

The Crystal Store is located in an attachment built onto the Print Shop. Candy, souvenirs, film, post cards, and ice cold drinks (chilled in a Rocky Mountain stream) can be purchased. The store is open for business Sunday through Friday. If the door is locked, one just honks his horn, and someone will come to assist the customer. The Treasure Mountain

Ranch Corporation owns and operates the store. It is closed on Saturday since this is their Sabbath Day.

The Norling Cabin...
When Joe Neal purchased this cabin in the early 1950's, it was fully furnished. The miners had left everything, including a Home Comfort woodstove, Victrola with records, bed, table and chairs, dishes, pots and pans, and silverware.

The Norling Cabin   Bonnie Neal photo

My wife Bonnie and I now reside in the Norling cabin. It is across the street from the Fogle cabin and was originally built in 1895.

Over the years I have been working on the restoration and repair of this cabin. My friends enjoy visiting me in Crystal and are always willing to assist with the many yearly projects. Jerry Youngman, Jim Hales, and Ken Ernsberger have helped with re-roofing, foundations, septic tank installation, and stovepipe replacements.

Our children, David and Joe Neal, also spend much of their vacation time in Crystal every summer and fall.

The School House…

There is no original date of construction listed in the Gunnison County Courthouse records for the schoolhouse. It is simply listed as "old." According to the *Edgerton Journal*, the construction of the school began on May 26, 1891 and was completed on June 19, 1891. The schoolhouse is currently undergoing renovation to make it into a residential cabin. The Treasure Mountain Ranch Corporation owns it. Following is an article that I wrote for the *Marble Chips* newsletter in November 2001. This is my recollection of yet another interesting event that occurred in Crystal.

Did You See the Martians?

In the fall of 1951, Theresa Francis was operating Ken's Pop Stand in Marble. Athos Willis, accompanied by a woman and her daughter, stopped by to talk to Theresa. Athos stated that he was headed to Crystal because the world was coming to an end. He believed Martians were going to flood the world below 9,000 feet. Athos Willis was planning to repopulate the world. Ms. Francis said he invited her to join them, but she said she really wasn't up to it.

Athos Willis and his two friends lived in the Crystal School House. Athos got cabin fever, and in mid-winter they trudged through the snow to Marble. They stopped at Charlie Orlosky's house. Willis asked Charlie to check on the supplies he had left in the schoolhouse.

Charlie agreed and that spring he went to Crystal. When he opened the schoolhouse door, a dog ran out. It was never seen again. According to Charlie, the dog had survived by eating raw potatoes.

When my family arrived in Marble that summer, Charlie gave us some bad news. The twin bridges, two miles below Crystal, had been blown up. Charlie had heard two explosions on the day Willis had stopped by his house. Now we would have to pack our supplies into Crystal. We had to fill our pillowcases with the supplies and make several trips.

Upon our arrival in Crystal we went to the schoolhouse to see what Athos Willis had left. It was truly amazing! Hanging on the walls were roller skates, a mink coat, power tools of all kinds, and a homemade crossbow with homemade arrows. The arrow tips were made from razor blades (the only thing that would kill Martians).

My brother and I were awestruck! My brother wanted to shoot the cross bow, and I wanted the hunting knife. Our parents told us to leave things alone because they didn't belong to us.

At one end of the schoolhouse there was an area approximately three feet high, four feet wide, and twelve feet long of written materials. Athos Willis had written articles about every subject imaginable. He had also drawn and colored charts of various emotions and their relationships to one another. Here is a sample of his writing: "It is 1952! Phew!! It stinks of rotten civilization!!!"; "This is the year the U.S.A. goes broke!!!! Then comes 1953!!!!!!! And May 10th!!!!!*

And this world runs out of time."; *"Nostradamus says 'People will shut their mouth to tell the truth'!!!!!"*

On Wednesday, August 31, 1955, Athos Willis made the news in the Rocky Mountain newspaper. He offered his body for sale. He stated that he would have to have time to spend the money and enjoy it before possession could occur.

Well, the next time you go to Crystal from Marble, look for the location of the old twin bridges. About 1 1/2 miles from Lizard Lake, you will come to the rockslide. As you begin up the rockslide, you will see the old road continue toward the river. This is where the first bridge was located. As you continue up the road, look to your right across the river and you can easily see the old roadbed. The second bridge was where an abandoned white truck rests at the bottom of the rockslide.

The School House   Concepta N. Waters photo

New Cabins in Crystal...

Dr. Richard Beamon owns the cabin at the west end of town on the right. Duane Fowler owns the cabin at the east end of town on the right.

At the end of each summer before the snow starts to fly in the fall, it is necessary to close our cabins and leave Crystal. Supplies are stored, windows shuttered, and cabins winterized. Following is a song written by Sharon Lodge Pitcher. Sharon grew up spending her summers in Crystal. It is a very special place for her as well as everyone who now resides here. Sharon was inspired to write this song after her brother, Denver experienced a lonely time in Crystal one winter.

SHARON'S SONG
We close up the cabins, gotta say good-bye
It's hard when you leave, not to break down and
cry
Cause you've had such a good time here this year
And it's hard to go, well, it's hard to go.

Say your good-byes and leave all your tears
And when you're far away and wishin' you were
here
Remember all these good times that I want
you to know
Yes, I want you to know.

That Crystal won't be Crystal without all its
friends
Crystal won't be Crystal, the way that it's been
It's sleeping beneath a blanket of snow
It's waiting for the springtime thaw

And Crystal can be Crystal again.

Well, Crystal's got a magic that I'm sure God gave
A magic that only God could have made
'Cause the friends that you make

And the memories you take

They will always stay, they will always stay

So fill your heart with all it can hold
Be a part of the stories later to be told
And when you're far away, I want you to know
Yes, I want you to know.

That Crystal won't be Crystal without all its
friends
Crystal won't be Crystal the way that it's been
It's sleeping beneath a blanket of snow
It's waiting for the springtime thaw.

Then Crystal can be Crystal again
Then Crystal can be Crystal again.

Accidents and Deaths. . .

It has been proven time and again that people must be aware of the many extreme dangers in this rugged mountain area. Those who do not respect these dangers risk losing their lives.

Hiker Drowns...
During the 1960's a group of young hikers from Ashcroft were coming down the trail from Lake Geneva. One of the hikers was lagging behind and took the wrong fork in the

trail. He tried to ford the river but was swept downstream by the strong current. Rescue parties and helicopters searched the area for several days. Finally, on the ninth day of the search his body was found in a logjam in the river. The rescuers used my father's chainsaw to remove the logs to get to his body.

Accidents at the Devil's Punch Bowls...

On August 19, 1967, Warren and Maxine Fowler with daughter Debbie and a friend, Jim Ashton of Ohio, were driving on the Schofield Road. Warren was driving his Scout; and as he approached the bridge at the Devil's Punch Bowls, he noticed there were people fishing underneath the bridge. In the split second that he took his eyes from the road, the Scout veered too close to the road edge and rolled off. It rolled down the embankment, landing on its side in the Crystal River. His passenger, Jim Ashton, was thrown against a boulder in the river, causing damage to his jaw and throat. Luckily, Debbie landed on top of Jim and was not injured. As I was hiking up the road, I met one of the fishermen on the road as he was running to Crystal for help. I immediately ran back to Crystal for help. My mom and a friend threw a mattress in the back of my dad's two wheel drive truck and drove to the scene of the accident. We placed Jim on the mattress and headed to Crystal where we met Carolyn Lodge. She told us that his neck was swelling from the throat contusions and that he would need to be taken to the emergency room in Glenwood Springs. We put cold compresses on his throat and drove as quickly as possible to Glenwood Springs. They did a tracheotomy and said he would need to be flown to Denver for further care. Jim was very fortunate. He survived this accident. Maxine and Warren were also very fortunate. They did not have any serious injuries, either.

Following are articles from the *Denver Post:*

(7-6-1970) "At the Punch Bowls, rain caused the bank to give way under a four-wheel drive Carry-All. It was going uphill with twelve passengers. The vehicle rolled backwards and over the bank. Nine people were killed."

(8-15-1971) "A Jeep was going downhill at the Devils Punch Bowls in two wheel drive. The driver tried to use the brakes to slow, but overheated, causing the jeep to go faster. It jumped out of gear and picked up more speed. The driver's wife jumped out and suffered a dislocated elbow. The driver and two children were killed. The vehicle rolled two and one-fourth times and ended against a large boulder four hundred yards below the Punch Bowls."

Accidents on Road to Snow Bridge...

Several accidents have occurred at approximately two miles above Crystal on the way to Schofield. Many of these have resulted in loss of life. At a point in the road where water continuously runs across a small crevice, vehicles have slipped off the wet rocks and plunged four hundred feet to the river valley below. Several vehicle bodies and other car parts can still be viewed from the road. If a person wishes to see these and not join them, he should park his car, get out, and look over the edge. People should not attempt to view the area from a moving vehicle, or they might end up there also! One of the accidents occurred in the late fall when the water had frozen. Two young men attempted to drive over the ice in their four wheel drive vehicle. The vehicle slid off the road and tumbled over the cliff. The driver was killed, and the passenger had a broken leg and wrist but managed to climb back to the road and made his way back to Crystal where he stayed in the Fogle house. When the young men did not arrive at their destination, a search party was sent. The young man in the Fogle cabin had kept warm by burning furniture in the woodstove until their arrival.

Man Swept over Falls...

In 1992 Ken Ramsey from Southwest City, Missouri, and friends were in Lead King Basin for a picnic. While getting a drink at the North Fork of the Crystal River, Chris Jones, a young boy, slipped on wet rocks and fell into the river just above the Coors Falls. Ken Ramsey immediately jumped into the river and pushed Chris back to safety, but Ken was swept over the rough, jagged rocks of the falls to a pool below. He was now on the opposite side of the river in a box canyon. His friends, not knowing how to get to him, rode an ATV to Crystal for help. Dr. Earl Beegle of Washington was visiting me. He and my sons, David and Joe, and I went to assist. We took a jeep to the falls and then drove across the bridge to the old mining road, which got us to the other side of the river. After hiking to the box canyon and rappelling down to the river, we were able to retrieve Ken. Dr. Beegle gave him medical attention. A word of caution - when near the Crystal River one should be very cautious about stepping on wet rocks because they are extremely slippery!

Two Men Killed in an Avalanche...

In January 1978 two young men were wintering in the Norling cabin. One of them was cross country skiing with a friend on Sheep Mountain. They were caught in a snowstorm and could not see because of a whiteout. They skied to the top of the mountain and were on the edge of a snow cornice, which gave way. Both plunged to their deaths from the resulting avalanche. When the search party discovered what happened, they decided to return in the spring to retrieve the bodies.

Climber Rescued on Snowmass Mountain...

During the early 1990's a doctor and his wife who were experienced climbers attempted to climb Snowmass Mountain from the southwest side. The man fell, breaking his leg and ribs. It was necessary for his wife to leave him on the mountain while she went for help. By the time a search party was notified, it was too late in the day to begin a search. The injured climber had to spend the cold night on the rocky slope alone. The next morning helicopters returned to the site, and he was retrieved and taken to a hospital where he recovered. Mountain climbing accidents occur each year in this wilderness area.

Accidents in the summer of 2004...

In the summer of 2004, a climber fell to his death, while descending from the summit of Snowmass Mountain.

A Jeep Rubicon drove too close to the edge of the Crystal road and rolled one hundred twenty-five feet down into the Crystal River.

149

Every summer someone tries to prove his four wheel drive vehicle can do something it is not capable of doing. Whether it's attempting to cross the snow bridge before the snow has melted, trying to drive up the road above the Punch Bowls, challenging the loop road when it is raining, or sightseeing while driving, accidents happen.

Roads in the Crystal Area . . .

In order to allow traffic to proceed to Crystal, snow avalanches must often be cleared from the road. In the springtime, bulldozers cut a path through fifteen or twenty foot deep avalanches. In springtime and early summer the road often floods due to the melting snow. The murky water can easily fool motorists. Sometimes it is deeper than expected, and the swift currents can wash a vehicle downstream. Disabled vehicles on the Crystal Road can expect to pay six hundred dollars or more to be rescued by a tow truck.

There are several common reasons vehicles are disabled on the road: flat tires, broken axles, cracked oil pans, and transmission failures. One example occurred when a rented 2001 Explorer arrived in Crystal with a flat tire.

The driver wanted to know if there was a filling station in town. I said, "Do you see that traffic light down the street?" After looking for a few seconds, he said, "Oh, I get it." (no electricity means no traffic lights). I was able to help him by plugging the tire and inflating it with Fix-A-Flat. He was able to continue to Carbondale and was very grateful. There are no auto services in Crystal or Marble. However, the residents are willing to provide assistance with minor emergency situations.

Some people are more daring than others. For two years in a row a motorist drove a brand new Cadillac from Schofield to Marble. The first time he came to Crystal, it was late at night. My father went outside, looked over his car, and asked if he needed help. The car was banged on both sides, and the muffler was missing. The motorist replied, "No, it's insured." The next year the same man brought another brand new Cadillac to Crystal from Schofield. It was in the same shape as the first, but he again said it was insured. He has not returned since, so I assume his insurance policy was canceled.

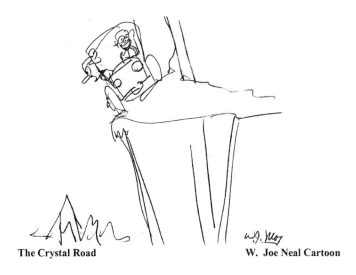

The Crystal Road   **W. Joe Neal Cartoon**

The Road from Marble to Crystal (forty-five minutes driving time)…

Approximately one-half mile from Beaver Lake, the road to Crystal begins at the bottom of Daniel's Hill. At this point, one will see the sign that states, "Four wheel drive vehicles." Hopefully, a person has a four wheel drive vehicle and can continue from this point to the top of Daniel's Hill, which is less than one mile long. At the top of the hill one takes the right branch. Crystal is four miles from this point. After a person passes Lizard Lake (named because of the salamanders that live in the lake), the road becomes very steep and drops down to the river level below. "Yes" is the answer to the question, "Does the road get worse?" As a person continues approximately one and one-fourth miles he will come to the rockslide area of the road. This is an extremely rough and narrow section of the road. Whoever has the closest passing point should use it, but a general rule is that drivers going uphill have the right-of-way. After crossing the rockslide, the road is rough but no longer dangerous. The Old Mill is two miles from the rockslide, and Crystal is just one-fourth mile farther. Crystal is at an altitude of 9,000 feet, and the views are simply breathtaking. John Darien kept the road in good repair from 1950 until his death in 1989. County Road 3, from Marble to Crystal, has steadily gone into disrepair since 1989. The road is much rougher than it was in 1950.

John Darien   Roger Neal collection

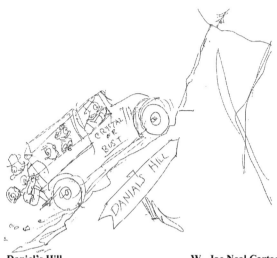

Daniel's Hill   W. Joe Neal Cartoon

The Loop Road (allow two hours)...

The Loop Road continues through Crystal to Lead King and back to Marble. The road traverses Mineral Point and Sheep Mountain and is even more narrow and rough than the road from Marble to Crystal. This is one of the most picturesque drives in the state of Colorado; however, it is also one of the most dangerous. Continuing out of Crystal approximately one-fourth mile, one takes the left branch in the road. One-half mile from this point after climbing a steep grade, he will take another left branch in the road. Lead King is three miles from Crystal. The driver should keep his eyes on the road when driving but will find it necessary to stop often to enjoy the scenery. Looking north from Lead King Basin a person can see views of Snowmass Mountain and Hagerman's Peak. One should also remember to look behind to see the snow basins of Treasure Mountain. The road will climb about two and one-half miles (A person shouldn't attempt this on a rainy day; the road turns to mud). At the top, beautiful mountain ranges and thick meadows of wildflowers can be seen. The entire loop road is about ten miles in length.

The Road to Schofield Park (allow one hour)...

There are sections of this road that are <u>extremely dangerous</u>. Following the road east out of Crystal, one takes the left fork and continues another one-half mile. After climbing a steep grade, one continues straight (the left fork goes to Lead King Basin). The snow bridge is about two and one-half miles from Crystal. An avalanche that occurs every winter forms this snow bridge. During normal snowfall winters the road is not open until mid July. If the road is open, the Devil's Punch Bowls are one-fourth mile ahead. Water cascades down the Crystal Canyon forming two waterfalls. The deep, round pools beneath these falls are called "The Devil's Punch Bowls." A person should park his vehicle before crossing the bridge and walk up the road to determine if he really wants to continue up this twenty-seven per cent grade. This one-fourth mile of the road is the most dangerous section. At the top of this shelf road, it will be necessary to ford the river. Schofield Park is one mile after the ford. Schofield Park is an open area that has lots of green meadows. One can continue on this road to Crested Butte, which is approximately twenty-five miles from Crystal.

Mountains in the Crystal Area...

The mountains which surround the town of Crystal are Sheep Mountain, Mineral Point, Big Bear Mountain, Little Bear Mountain, Crystal Peak, and Treasure Mountain. Other mountains near Crystal are Treasury Mountain, Galena Mountain, Snowmass Mountain, and Hagerman's Peak.

Galena, Treasure and Treasury...
These mountains are all connected. A mine is located within one hundred feet from the top of Galena Mountain. The old mining shack is still standing, and galena ore is scattered nearby. A saddle ridge connects Galena and Treasury, and both can easily be climbed in one day. Treasure Mountain is the highest and can be climbed from Yule Lakes. The Yule Lakes are on the southwest slope of the mountain. Fishing is very good at Yule Lakes.

Sheep Mountain   Bonnie Neal photo

Sheep Mountain...

The road from Lizard Lake to Crystal was carved out of the side of Sheep Mountain by the pioneers in the 1880's. The Crystal River flows at the base of this mountain. Some of the best known mines on this mountain are the Black Queen, Black Eagle, Sheep Mountain Tunnel, Lucky Boy, Catalpa, and Inez. For those interested in climbing this mountain, there is a road on the gentle northwest slope that goes to the top. For the more adventurous and experienced climbers, the cliff faces on the west and north are a challenge.

Mineral Point   Bonnie Neal photo

Mineral Point...

As seen from Crystal, this mountain is the top of a steep cliff between the North Fork River and the Crystal River. Some of the best known mines located on this mountain are the Daisy, Belle of Titusville, and Whopper. This mountain can be climbed by using two trails. Ulysses S. Grant named the SOB trail after riding a burro over the trail from Schofield. The SOB trail is located about one mile west of the snow bridge. Another trail is an old mining trail located in Lead King Basin. Both trails are not well marked and are difficult to find. The more experienced climber can also scale the cliffs of the mountain.

Crystal Peak   Bonnie Neal photo

Crystal Peak...

An important mine on this peak was the Crystal Mountain Tunnel. This is one of the easier mountains to climb. It can be climbed easily from Schofield by going through the North Pole Basin on the east side. A more challenging climb would be from the Crystal side. This mountain has an altitude of 12,632 feet. I have climbed this mountain many times, but the most exciting time occurred when we saw a mother wolverine with her two young as we were descending the mountain.

Big Bear and Little Bear...

These mountains are mostly forest covered and are connected. Bear Mountain Tunnel is the most notable mine on Big Bear.

159

The Starlight Campground was located on the west side at the foot of Big Bear Mountain.

Bear Mountain   Bonnie Neal photo

Hagerman's Peak and Snowmass Mountain...

A thin razor sharp ridge connects these mountains. Hagerman's Peak is 13,831 feet, and Snowmass is 14,092 feet. Both are considered a challenge to climb from the south side. Both mountains are composed of loose, crumbly granite. To climb Hagerman's Peak, beginning climbers should plan to camp overnight at Lake Geneva. They should plan to begin their climb early in the morning so that they can be descending the mountaintop by noon. Rain, snow, and sleet are common on this mountain at anytime of the day or year. Climbers should follow the south ridge and cross over to the east ridge, then follow this east ridge to the top.

Snowmass Mountain and Hagerman's Peak   Roger Neal collection

During the summer of 1971 my friend, Ken Hauser, and I were attempting to climb Hagerman's Peak for the first time to honor my father's wishes of having his ashes scattered on this mountain. It was raining; my friend was not accustomed to the altitude and got mountain sickness. We did not have enough food because we each thought the other had brought the food. After we had completed about one-third of the climb, my friend thought it was too dangerous and decided not to continue. I attempted to continue the climb alone; but due to a storm and my exhaustion, I chose to scatter the ashes on the mountainside approximately three hundred feet

161

from the top. I figured my Dad wouldn't want me to kill myself in the process of scattering his ashes. The next year I was determined to reach the top of this mountain. Three friends and I planned to climb, but they decided after spending the night at Lake Geneva, they would not be able to continue. I told them to watch for a mirror flash from the top and began the climb. As time passed, it began to get cloudy; and at several points, I heard thunder. I began climbing really fast in order to beat the rain. Every time I stopped to rest, I heard the thunder. Finally, after resting, I realized it was the rumble of my stomach and not thunder. I continued climbing and was elated to reach the summit with no major problems. Since then, I have climbed this mountain two times. The second time was the summer of 1982 with my friend, Ron Stern, and his son, Carey. We left from Lead King Basin and were back in Crystal by six that evening. In 1986 I climbed with my son's Boy Scout troop. The five of us made it to the top with no major difficulties. On the descent we started down a steep snow bank. The lead climber lost his footing and slid about one hundred fifty feet to a boulder field. He managed to stop himself and waited at the bottom to stop each climber as he slid down.

Snowmass Mountain is usually climbed one of two ways from Lead King Basin. Most climbers camp at Lake Geneva. The next morning they climb the S-Ridge that ends at the north end of the lake. This is the route Mario Villalobos and I used when we attempted to climb Snowmass in 1993. The first climb is where most people make their mistakes; and our mistake was to begin our climb from Lead King Basin instead of Lake Geneva. We reached the base of the mountain at 9:30 a.m. At 12:30 p.m. we were only halfway up the S-Ridge when a thunderstorm began. We started down as quickly as possible but kept hearing a buzzing noise. I asked Mario what the noise was, and he said it was the metal bead on top of his baseball cap. He took his cap off and his hair was standing straight up from the static electricity. I then felt a smack on my head and realized the nylon hood on my jacket was also conducting electricity. We got off the ridge as quickly as possible and felt lucky to make it down the mountain safely.

My second climb was with my son Joe on September 6, 2001. I decided we would try to climb Snowmass, leaving from Little Gem Lake. This lake is on the northwest side of Snowmass and is approximately eight hundred feet higher than Lake Geneva. We camped at the lake and the next morning started our climb at 8:00 a.m. I found climbing from this side much easier because we were closer to the summit, and the rock climbing was not so challenging. It was very cold, and wind gusts were up to 40 m.p.h. If we'd had the foresight to bring gloves, I could have avoided getting frostbitten fingers. We reached the summit at 11:30 a.m., took our pictures, signed our names in the registration cylinder, made cellular phone calls, ate lunch, and started our descent by noon. We arrived back at camp in two hours, just as it began to hail. This was a great accomplishment for my son and me, and the experience of climbing together is a treasured memory.

Day Hiking from Crystal . . .

When going on a day hike, one should plan to take a camera, rain poncho, water, light lunch or snack, hard candy or gum (keeps mouth from getting dry), insect lotion, and sunscreen.

Some of the shortest hikes would include the Old Mill, Crystal Falls, Patricia Falls, Schoolhouse, and the Inez Mine.

The Old Mill...

It is located one-fourth mile southwest of Crystal. This is a favorite site for artists and photographers. It has been painted and photographed so often that it is widely known throughout the country. Residents sometimes swim in the Old Mill Pond, and fishermen often test their skills in the pond. For this reason, one should avoid the temptation of tossing rocks into the water.

Crystal Falls...

This falls is nestled in a grove of trees, where the water tumbles down the rocky, moss-covered rocks to a beaver pond below. It is another beautiful location for photographs, so one should remember to take his camera.

Patricia Falls...

Patricia Falls (formerly Inez Falls) is located north of Crystal on the North Fork River. This sixty foot falls thunders down the rocky canyon walls, creating a fine spray of mist. The best time to get a picture of this falls is between noon and 3:00 p.m. when the sun shines directly on the falls, causing rainbows through the mist.

Patricia Falls   Roger Neal collection

The following scenic day hikes begin from Crystal. One should follow the road west to the fork and stay left. There will be a steep grade before coming to a second fork. The left fork goes to Lead King Basin, and the right goes to Schofield.

Lead King Basin...
This is a three mile hike. The road has several switchbacks on Mineral Point. From this road one will be able to take a photograph of the town far below. A person should enjoy this hike at a leisurely pace and take pleasure in the many panoramic views. When in the basin, the valley opens up. The Treasure Mountain range can be seen to the south. To the north are Hagerman's Peak and Snowmass Mountain. One can test his skills in locating the Lead King Mine with its black and gray mine dump. This mine is on private property but can be viewed from the road. Looking up and to the left in the aspen trees, one will see the mine in the middle of this hill. Many beautiful flowers carpet this valley floor.

Lake Geneva...
After arriving in Lead King Basin, a person should continue on the road across the bridge past the Forest Service parking lot. It is easy to miss the trailhead. After one crosses Silver Creek, the trail will be about one hundred

feet on the right just before an aspen grove. One should follow this trail three-fourths mile to a fork and stay left. This is a very steep two mile climb, which seems like four miles. While one is climbing the trail, Maroon Bells can be seen to the east. When one arrives at the beaver ponds the lake is less than one half mile away.

Little Gem Lake (for the avid hiker)...

To reach Little Gem, one should follow the trail on the west side of Lake Geneva. Little Gem is above timberline, approximately two miles farther. This is really a pond nestled on a ridge surrounded by alpine grasses. The vista from this location is breathtaking. Many climbers use this point to begin their ascension of Snowmass Mountain.

Lake Siberia (for the avid hiker)...

One continues from Little Gem Lake approximately one mile to the boulder-covered surroundings of Lake Siberia. This desolate lake has been appropriately named Lake Siberia.

Schofield Road...

To get to the Snow Bridge, Devil's Punch Bowls, and Schofield Park one should see the directions under *The Roads to Crystal.*

Fishing Adventures . . .

My first fishing experience in Crystal was with my older brother. I was eight years old and did not have a fishing pole. He had a fiberglass rod and was fishing in a beaver pond. Not having a pole, I walked down stream and noticed several fish swim under a bank when they saw me. Lying down on the bank, I slowly extended my arm under it. I touched a trout, and it did not move. Gently, I put my hand around the trout's body and gradually squeezed until I could bring it out of the water. I continued doing this until I had about five or six trout. My brother saw all the trout I had caught and tried to catch some as I had done. He became disgusted when he was not successful, threw his pole into the beaver pond, and left. I waded out into the pond to retrieve the pole, and that's how I got my first fishing pole.

I was very excited about having my very own pole and went fishing in the rivers, beaver ponds, and lakes often. I quickly learned that if trout saw me, they schooled-up, moved to another area in the water, and refused to bite. One advantage I had was that I could see trout in a swiftly moving stream, but they couldn't see me. When fishing in calm waters, I learned to sneak up on the fish by crawling on my hands and knees and then casting into the pool. My favorite fishing area was Rock Creek (now known as the North Fork of the Crystal River). During the snowmelt in the spring this river becomes a raging torrent. The river turns to a chocolate brown color and churns wildly downstream. The fish would be in small pools and again could not see me due to the murky water. Fishing was great, but I often slipped on the wet rocks, fell into the river, and lost my pole. After falling in, I would go home, soaking wet and crying my eyes out because I had lost my pole. Getting a string and grappling hook, my mother would follow me back to the place where I had lost the pole. Usually, she was successful in retrieving the pole. Once, when we were not successful, I began using a willow for my pole. This was during a time when Doc A. T. Waski first came to Crystal. He was outfitted with hip waders, fly fishing vest, fishing hat decorated with an assortment of flies, wicker creel, and the nicest fly fishing rod and reel I had ever seen. I was extremely impressed and thought Doc must be a great fisherman. When he asked my dad where to go fishing, my dad told him, "Just ask Roger; he knows where the trout are." I took Doc down to Rock Creek and pointed out a trout; but he couldn't see it, so I told him where to drop his bait. After fishing that particular spot for several minutes with no luck, I asked if I could try with my willow pole. He said, "Sure, go ahead. I don't think there are any fish in there." On the first cast I caught the trout. He was dumbfounded that a twirpy little kid could catch a trout using a willow pole. We walked back to the cabin; and after telling my dad the story, he said, "Roger, I think you're going to get more use out of this than I am," and he gave me his rod and reel.

We had many trout meals at our table. When I went fishing, my mother often told me how many fish to catch. One day we had company, and she asked me to catch several fish. I caught well over the limit. While my mother was preparing to bread the fish, two game wardens came through town on horseback. My mother ran to the door and yelled for them to come see the fish I had caught. I knew they were going to send me to jail for catching so many trout, so I ran out the back door. After they left, my mother told me they just said, "Be sure you eat all of them." I was very relieved that they weren't going to put me in jail.

Roger with catch   Roger Neal collection

Ken Hauser, an avid fisherman from Indiana, visited me in Crystal. Ken had been listening to my "fishing tales" for years and wanted to go fishing in the Crystal River near the snow bridge. I knew where there was a pool with a sixteen inch trout. I told Ken where to fish, and he hooked the trout. The problem was he was standing knee deep in water, and there was nowhere to land it. While reeling in the trout, it began swimming around and around his legs. I told him to just use his cowboy hat for a net. He "hatted" the sixteen inch trout, but the hat shrank dramatically. His hat now is a wall decoration in my cabin and a reminder of "the one that almost got away."

My father never had an interest in fishing until later in life. He enjoyed hiking and painting in his spare time. However, during the

171

last ten years of his life, he became a very good fisherman. As a young boy I can remember his carrying me on his shoulders when we went on hikes, but we never went fishing together. The only fishing experience I remember with my father occurred when we were fishing up the canyon near Lead King Basin. My father was in poor health and very frail. He wanted to cross the river to fish a pool but was concerned about slipping on the rocks and falling. I told him to get on my back and I would carry him across. He got on my back; and as we were crossing, he reminded me several times, "Don't fall." After fishing the pool, we crossed again; and this was probably the saddest fishing experience I have ever had. Instead of my father carrying me, I was now carrying my father. Two years later my father died, and this is a memory I will never forget.

Where to catch trout...

Since the Crystal River has not been stocked since 1997, the best places to fish are Beaver Lake and the Crystal River below Marble. Geneva Lake has plenty of fish, but they are difficult to catch. The water is so clear the fish can see the fisherman and will refuse to bite.

Good Times in Crystal . . .

Every fall in the 1950's and early 1960's a "Wing-Ding" was held at the Crystal Club. Everyone in the valley, including Schofield, Marble, and Ragged Mountain Ranch was invited. Lee Sperry, of Ragged Mountain Ranch, provided a sheep that was roasted on a spit over hot coals. Dick Car-Skaden always prepared his famous spaghetti, and I provided fresh Rocky Mountain trout. Everyone brought a favorite food to share. There was music, singing, and dancing; and all had a great time.

Daily adventures included hiking, fishing, mountain climbing, and mine exploration. Of course, there was always plenty of time for reading books and magazines. Nightly activities included playing Monopoly, Yahtzee, Rook, Password, and various other board games. My mother, Fogle, enjoyed debating the pros and cons of past and present political decisions. These activities often lasted late into the night.

Roger making ice cream   Roger Neal collection

Today, when people come to Crystal, they often ask, "What do you do for fun up here? You don't have electricity, television, telephones, newspaper, or mail delivery." Some of the best times in Crystal are gathering around campfires with good friends, roasting hot dogs and marshmallows, singing songs, and telling stories. Birthdays are often celebrated with cake and homemade ice cream made by using snow from the snow bridge. The entire Crystal population is invited to these celebrations. We still enjoy board games, cards, and reading. A good game of volleyball, wiffleball, softball or horseshoe is not uncommon. The Crystal horseshoe champion, Ken Gray, is always looking for a challenge.

The sport of mountain biking is an adventure enjoyed by many. The mountain biker can see the same scenic sites as those riding in a standard four-wheel drive vehicle in approximately the same amount of time.

ATV adventures are the newest outdoor activity. The ATV allows a person to go to areas in a shorter amount of time than when hiking or driving a standard four wheel drive vehicle. Like all other motorized vehicles, ATV's are not allowed on hiking trails.

Safety equipment is always advised when one goes mountain climbing, mountain biking, or on an ATV adventure.

Keith Lindquist from Southwest City, Missouri, has visited Crystal often. He, too, fell in love with Crystal and has written the following cowboy poem. This poem does an outstanding job of describing this unique little town of Crystal and its close-knit community of very special people.

CRYSTAL, COLORADO

I've got this little story to tell; some people
they may call it a ditty.
It's about the most beautiful place on
Earth, a place called Crystal City.
Well, it's a lovely mountain setting, and it
lays at 9,000 feet,
It's probably the only place on Earth that's
got boulders in the middle of Main
Street.
Well, it's a long and treacherous road to
get to this little town.
And when you come by Lizard Lake, Lord,
it's a long ways down.
As you continue on this trail that the
natives call a road,
You wonder all the time how much further
can this thing go.
And as you still continue on and begin to
build a little esteem,
Your wife beside you in the truck, lets out
this blood-curdling scream.
She says, "Get over! Get away from the
edge! There's a car body down below!
Please, honey, let's turn back! We don't
really have to go!"
Well, we kinda talked it over and I settled
her down. And with both hands on the
wheel,

I popped that next little grade and there it was, The Mill.
We just kinda sat there in awe and marveled at all the sights.
And we realized this view of the Mill was worth all the many frights.
Well, I could end this story here, but it would be quite incomplete.
Because around this corner and up this hill, there's some people you have got to meet.
Now there are so many personalities here that I hate to just name a few,
But if I didn't I'd be cheating them; and I'd sure enough be cheating you.
Now, right over there; that's Roger, the Story Teller. That's what he is known as around these parts.
He can tell you stories that could scare you to death or stories that could win your heart.
It doesn't matter what cabin your staying in, he'll tell you there's a monster that lives under the floor.
And when he gets through telling you the first one, you'll ask him to just tell you one more.
Now there's Dail, Carolyn and Dorothy their kinda mainstay around this town.
I know it's true, what I am telling you, because people come to see them from

177

miles around.
Then there's Carl G. That's what he is
known to you and me cause nobody
can pronounce his last name.
The neat thing about Carl G is that his
personality is always the same.
Come daylight hours, he might get out his
photographs and try to make a little
cash.
But come night around the dinner table,
he'll give us heck at Balderdash.
Bonnie and Leland Stanford, oohhhh, their
as sweet as they can be.
How do you get to their place? Well, just
come and follow me.
It's up this little trail and down the other
side.
It's the first place on the left: knock before
you go inside.
If you want to talk cars and trains, Leland
knows them from inside out.
And if you want the best cinnamon rolls in
the world, they're Bonnie's-There is no
doubt.
Well, I'd like to thank you for your
attention.
But let me make one thing clear enough to
see.
If you ever come to Crystal include Friday
nights. 'Cause Friday nights are free.

APPENDIX

THE PEOPLE OF CRYSTAL
(1938-2005)

Emmet S. Gould (deceased)

Helen Gould Collins (deceased)

Maxine Collins Fowler, Warren Fowler (both deceased)
2nd m Cora Fowler
Duane (Dorothy) Fowler
Amy Geneva Fowler
Jeremy (Mari Rendon) Fowler
John Jeremy Fowler
Gabriel Santiago Fowler
Jeremy Edwin Fowler
Larissa Kimberly Fowler
Debbie Fowler Heise and Steve Heise
Miranda Heise
Luke Heise
Carolyn Collins Lodge and Dr. Dail Lodge
Dail, Jr., (Hannacho) Lodge
Jason Lodge
Jennifer Lodge Clark and
Jon Clark
Denver Lodge
Candace Lodge
Weston Lodge
Sharon Lodge Pitcher and Dale Pitcher
Caleb Tyler Pitcher

Dorothy Gould Tidwell and Spencer Tidwell
(both deceased)
Marilyn Tidwell Cox (deceased)

179

Appendix

Chris (Rachel) Cox
    Joshua Cox
    Jonathan Cox
    Daniel Cox
Cindy Cox Jones

Welcome Joe Neal and Esther Fogle Neal (both deceased)
    Patricia Neal Gray and Kenneth E. Gray
        Jefferson M. Gray
        Douglas H. (Julie) Gray
            Madison Gray
            Abigail Gray
    Joe David Neal
    Roger A. Neal and Bonnie Neal
        David A. Neal
        Joe B. Neal

Frank Reh (deceased) and Emily Reh (deceased)

Richard Car-Skaden (deceased)

Theodore Jackson (deceased)

Charles Bassett (deceased) and Gladys Bassett (deceased)

Albert Erhard (deceased) and Conny Erhard
    George Erhard
    Eben (Lori) Erhard

Leland Stanford (deceased) and Bonnie Stanford

Dr. Rob Anderson and Manette Anderson
    Brynne Anderson

Appendix

Tays Anderson
Riley Anderson

Dr. Richard Beamon and Andi Beamon

BIBLIOGRAPHY

BOOKS

Bancroft, Caroline, *Unique Ghost Towns and Mountain Spots,* Johnson Publishing Co., Boulder, Co., 1961.

Collman, Russ, and McCoy, Dell, *The Crystal River Pictorial,* Sundance Ltd., Denver, Co., 1972.

Francis, Theresa V., *Crystal River Saga,* Marble, Co., Privately Printed, 1959.

Houston, Robert B., Jr., *The Battle Over Silver: Porter Nelson in Aspen,* Professional Press, Nov. 1996.

Jack, Ellen E., *Fate of a Fairy,* W. B. Conkey Company, Chicago, IL, 1910.

McCollum, Jr., Oscar, *Marble, A Town Built on Dreams, Vol. I,* Sundance Publications, Ltd., Denver, Co., 1972.

Myers, Rex C., and Vandenbusche, Duane, *Marble, Colorado: City of Stone,* Golden Bell Press, Denver, Co., 1972.

Vandenbusche, Duane, *The Gunnison Country,* B & B Printers, Gunnison, Inc., Gunnison, Co., 1980.

Williams, John P., *A History of the Horace H. Williams Family,* Privately Printed, 1980.

Bibliography

BUSINESSES AND INSTITUTIONS

Colorado Historical Society, Denver, Colorado.

Elkhart Public Library, Elkhart, Indiana.

Leslie Savage Library, Western State College, Gunnison, Colorado.

Levine, Brian, *Mt. Gothic Tomes and Reliquary Rare Books Western America*, www.mtgothictomes.com.

Marble Historical Society, Marble, Colorado.

Moyer, Cheri, First Gunnison Title and Escrow, Gunnison, Colorado.

NEWSPAPERS

Denver Post, (Denver), August 15, 1971.

Gunnison News-Democrat, (Gunnison), June 24, 1881.

The Crystal River Current, (Crystal), October 2, 1886 – September 24, 1887.

The Silver Lance, (Crystal), July 16, 1897 – October 20, 1899.

Valley Journal, (Carbondale), September 1984.

183

Bibliography

PUBLIC DOCUMENTS

Edgerton, Frank and Rose D., *The Edgerton Journal,* Colorado Historical Society, Denver, Colorado, 1886-1895.

Geological Survey Bulletin 884, U. S. Dept. of Interior.

Mining Patents, Ute Series Mineral Certificates, Rock Creek Mining District, Gunnison County Clerk's Office, Gunnison, Colorado.

Vanderwilt, John W., *Geology and Mineral Deposits of the Snowmass Mountain Area*, Gunnison County, Gunnison, Colorado

PERSONAL INTERVIEWS

Anderson, Dr. Rob and Manette, Glenwood Springs, Colorado, February 2002.

Blue, June, Marble, Colorado, July 2003.

Brown, Wayne, Marble, Colorado, January 2002.

Cox, Chris, Kamuela, Hawaii, February 2002.

Earhart, Robert, Aurora, Colorado, January 2002.

Erhard, Conny, San Manuel, Arizona, February 2002.

Fortsch, Mark, Las Vegas, Nevada, September 2001.

Bibliography

Fowler, Duane, Denver, Colorado, February 22, 2002, March 3, 2002.

Fowler, Warren, Riverside, California, January 2002.

Gray, Patricia Neal, Charlottesville, Virginia, December 2001, January 2002, February 2002.

Heise, Debbie, Riverside, California, February 2002.

Hogue, Aileen M., Chestertown, Maryland, January 2002, March 2002.

Houston, Robert B., Jr., Arlington, Virginia, November 2004.

Lodge, Dr. Dail and Carolyn, Lake Havasu, Arizona, December 2001, January 2002, February 2002, March 4, 2002.

McCollum, Jr., Oscar, Marble, Colorado, January 2002.

Neal, Joe David, Mooresville, Indiana, February 2002, April 2002.

Orlosky, Jack, Marble, Colorado, September 2001.

Robinson, William, Colorado Springs, Colorado, January 2002, February 2002.

Sperry, Joe, Somerset, Colorado, March 3, 2002.

Bibliography

Stanford, Bonnie, Southwest City, Missouri, February 2002.

Swanson, Robert, Aurora, Colorado, December 2001.

Villalobos, Mario, Marble, Colorado, March 3, 2002.

Williams, Andrew, Merced, California, January 2002.

Williams, John, Tucson, Arizona, January 2002.

INDEX
[* - photo or sketch]